Catholicism

Other Books in the Religions and Religious Movements series:

Buddhism

Christianity

Confucianism

Hinduism

Islam

Judaism

Shinto

Catholicism

Maria L. Howell, Book Editor

GREENHAVEN PRESS

An imprint of Thomson Gale, a part of The Thomson Corporation

Detroit • New York • San Francisco • New Haven, Conn. • Waterville, Maine • London

THOMSON

———✦———™

GALE

Christine Nasso, *Publisher*
Elizabeth Des Chenes, *Managing Editor*

© 2007 Thomson Gale, a part of The Thomson Corporation.

Thomson and Star logo are trademarks and Gale and Greenhaven Press are registered trademarks used herein under license.

For more information, contact:
Greenhaven Press
27500 Drake Rd.
Farmington Hills, MI 48331-3535
Or you can visit our Internet site at http://www.gale.com

ISBN-13: 978-0-7377-3511-6
ISBN-10: 0-7377-3511-2

Library of Congress Control Number: 2006938250

Printed in the United States of America
10 9 8 7 6 5 4 3 2 1

Contents

Chapter 1: The Origins of Catholicism

Chapter 2: The Evolution of the Church

Chapter 3: The Catholic Church in the Twentieth Century

Chapter 4: Contemporary Developments and Debates

Foreword

*"Religion . . . is not really what is grasped
by the brain. It is a heart grasp."*
        —Mohandas Gandhi

The impulse toward religion—to move beyond the world as we know it and ponder the larger questions of why we are here, whether there is a God who directs our lives, and how we should live—seems as universally human as breathing.

Yet, although this impulse is universal, different religions and their adherents are often at odds due to conflicts that stem from their opposing belief systems. These conflicts can also occur because many people have only the most tentative understanding of religions other than their own. In a time when religion seems to be at the root of growing tensions around the world, its study seems particularly relevant.

We live in a religiously diverse world. And while the world's many religions have coexisted for millennia, only recently, with information shared so easily and travel to even the most remote regions made possible for larger numbers of people, has this fact been fully acknowledged. It is no longer possible to ignore other religions, regardless of whether one views these religions positively or negatively.

The study of religion has also changed a great deal in recent times. Just a few decades ago in the United States, few students were exposed to any religion other than Christianity. Today, the study of religion reflects the pluralism of American society and the world at large. Religion courses and even current events classes focus on non-Christian religions as well as the religious experiences of groups that have in the past been marginalized by traditional Christianity, such as women and racial minorities.

In fact, the study of religion has been integrated into many different types of classes and disciplines. Anthropology, psychology, sociology, history, philosophy, political science, economics, and other fields often include discussions about different nations' religions and beliefs.

The study of religion involves so many disciplines because, for many cultures, it is integrated into many different parts of life. This point is often highlighted when American companies conduct business deals in Middle Eastern countries and inadvertently offend a host country's religious constrictions, for example. On both a small scale, such as personal travel, and on a large scale, such as international trade and politics, an understanding of the world's religions has become essential.

The goals of the Religions and Religious Movements series are several. The first is to provide students a historical context for each of the world's religions. Each book focuses on one religion and explores, through primary and secondary sources, its fundamental belief system, religious works of importance, and prominent figures. By using articles from a variety of sources, each book provides students with different theological and historical contexts for the religion.

The second goal of the series is to explore the challenges that each religion faces today. All of these religions are experiencing challenges and changes—some theological, some political—that are forcing alterations in attitude and belief. By reading about these current dilemmas, students will come to understand that religions are not abstract concepts, but a vital part of peoples' lives.

The last and perhaps most important objective is to make students aware of the wide variety of religious beliefs, as well as the factors, common to all religions. Every religion attempts to puzzle out essential questions as well as provide a model for doing good in the world. By using the books in the Religions and Religious Movements series, students will find that people with divergent, closely held beliefs may learn to live together and work toward the same goals.

Introduction

Marie is a Catholic school teacher with three teenage children. Her youngest daughter, Sherrie, dreams of becoming a Catholic priest. Each time she mentions her desire to a priest at her local church, she is told "I'm sorry, Sherrie, but that's just not possible." Marie believes that the leadership of the Catholic church is simply biased toward women, and out of step with the modern world. "Catholicism is very, very man based," she states, "because men run the church; the Pope is a man; the cardinals, the bishops, and priests are men . . . everybody in leadership is a man! I think that we're all here to work together as equals. It's not men up there judging women down here."

Marie's resentment and anger toward the organization and hierarchical nature of the Catholic church is not unusual: Her feelings are symptomatic of the underlying division and debate within the church today. Although the fundamental teachings of the church have remained the same throughout its 2,000-year history, the changes initiated by the Second Vatican Council (1962–1965) with regard to the church's traditions, rituals, and practices have given rise to a great polarization within the church itself. In addition to the issue of women's ordination, many Catholics are divided over the question of the traditions of the liturgy and the debate over whether priests should continue to be required to be celibate. Some Catholics argue that the church is out of step with the modern world and that the changes have not gone far enough, while others contend that the church should hold firmly to its tradition and resist any modifications that would dilute the essence of its original teachings.

The Language of the Church

In the "Constitution on the Sacred Liturgy" promulgated by Pope Paul VI in 1963, the Second Vatican Council, commonly known as Vatican II, stated that it would be a great advantage to offer Mass offered in the native language of each country. It was a way for all Catholics to become active participants in the prayers and responses of the Mass. Most Masses today are conducted in the language of the people—a change that many Catholics welcomed and believed was long overdue but that others disagree with. Some argue that in replacing Latin with the vernacular as the language of the Mass, the church has lost part of its identity that was distinctly and uniquely Catholic. According to Bob O'Gorman and Mary Faulkner, the authors of *Understanding Catholicism*, before Vatican II, Catholics could travel to any major city in the world and feel at home when attending Mass because they would hear the same prayers being said in the same manner as they were said in their hometown. Some Catholics felt that the use of the vernacular caused a deep loss of church tradition and rituals that once formed the core of many Catholics' spiritual and social lives and symbolized. On the other hand, many Catholics feel that the changes brought about by Vatican II in the language of the liturgy brought the church more in line with the modern world and made the content of the ceremonies more understandable to the congregations. Although Vatican II took place more than four decades ago, the debate over the language of the services continues to be heated.

Women in the Church

No issue is more divisive among Catholics than women's ordination. According to current church law, only men may receive sacred ordination. Sister Butler of the Mundelein Seminary in Illinois argues that tradition dictates male-only priesthood:

> Catholics have always insisted that the ordained ministry has its origin in Jesus's choice of the Twelve [Apostles] and that they are the foundation of the Church. [In the] second and third centuries some people went ahead and admitted

women to at least priestly functions, if not to ordination, and those people were considered heretics. The response was that this was not what Christ willed, and it's against apostolic teaching. . . . We don't think Jesus intended [female ordination], and this judgment has been made repeatedly and definitively by the church of our own ancestors. It's a universal, unbroken tradition.

In addition, Catholics who support the male-only priesthood argue that priesthood isn't a "job" but a vocation or calling by God. As Deacon Keith Fournier writes, "Priesthood is not about a 'right' or even a 'career' but rather, it is a response to a 'vocation,' where the one responding hears the voice . . . of the Holy Spirit to uniquely follow and re-present Jesus Christ, God Incarnate, who came among us as a man . . . not because men are somehow 'better' but because He initiated God's gift and redemptive action of love among us."

However, many argue that women should indeed be allowed to be ordained as priests and in other leadership roles in the Catholic church. Some theologians state that at issue is the question of equality and that not permitting women to be ordained creates two classes of baptism, thereby violating St. Paul's statement that everyone is equal in Christ. Furthermore, others refute the argument that Catholic tradition dictates that only men can serve as priests, pointing out that in antiquity, in fact some women were ordained as priests and bishops. Finally, some advocates of female ordination offer a pragmatic argument in favor of allowing women to serve as priests, stating that because the numbers of men who feel called to the priesthood in Europe and North America are declining, there aren't enough clergy to administer the Sacraments in these regions. They argue that women who feel called to serve God should therefore be allowed to fulfill this role.

Celibacy in the Church

According to church tradition, priests (and nuns) make a vow of lifetime celibacy as part of their commitment to God and their sacred calling. In his letter *Pastores Dabo Vobis* (I Will Give You Shepherds) Pope John Paul II reaffirmed the celibate role of priests writing that by virtue of their ordination, priests have "marrie[d]" to the Church because the Church (the parishioners—men, women and children) is seen as the "Bride of Christ." However, celibacy has become controversial among Catholics and others for at least two reasons. First, as theologians John Trigilio and Kenneth Brighenti discuss, many Catholics believe the decline in the number of priests in the Catholic church is due primarily to the fact that ordained priests must remain celibate. They believe that it's time for the church to reconsider allowing married men to serve as priests. As practicing Catholic Kenneth Carcaterra writes,

> There are many good men in the Church who would become priest if the Church allowed married men to be ordained. . . . In the Eastern Catholic Church there is precedent for allowing married men to be ordained. . . . In the Latin Church (the Roman Rite) married men could be ordained as diocesan priests, working on the front lines of our communities. Having spouses and families one could argue they would be more in touch with the faithful, better understanding the day to day trials and tribulations. Celibacy can (and should) remain a part of the Catholic priesthood, but can be reserved for the religious orders (i.e. Dominicans, Franciscans, etc.) or as a personal choice.

On the other hand, others argue that there is little evidence to support this argument against required celibacy in the church. Deacon Fournier writes, "Celibacy is not the source of the purported 'shortage' of priests. If one were to examine the trends, there is a growing response to the call to the celibate priesthood where the Catholic faith is being faithfully lived and courageously demonstrated. . . . rather than a problem, celibacy is a gift and unique vocation."

In addition, some Catholics feel that the recently reported widespread sexual abuse of young boys was caused in part by the celibate nature of the priesthood; and some have even argued that the church should allow priests to marry in order to solve the problem of pedophilia among Catholic priests in the United States and elsewhere. However, the church leadership maintains that the sexual abuse wasn't caused by celibacy but by a failure of the priests to adhere to the teachings of Christ and poor seminary guidance. Church representative also point out that the majority of priests do not commit sex crimes and cite research that shows no correlation between celibacy and sexual abuse. For example, in his article "The Myth of the Pedophile Priest," scholar Philip Jenkins writes, "My research of cases over the past 20 years indicates no evidence whatever that Catholic or other celibate clergy are any more likely to be involved in misconduct or abuse than clergy of any other denomination—or indeed, than nonclergy. However determined news media may be to see this affair as a crisis of celibacy, the charge is just unsupported."

The debates over the liturgy, the ordination of women, and celibacy are just a few of the important issues in the history of the Catholic church. In *Catholicism*, the authors present a variety of perspectives on the Roman Catholic Church, including its origins in the Jewish faith, its role during times of war, and contemporary developments and controversies.

CHAPTER 1

The Origins
of Catholicism

The Source of Christianity

John C. Dwyer

John C. Dwyer is a graduate of Fordham and Georgetown universities. He also holds a doctorate in theology from the University of Tubingen, Germany. He served for many years as professor of theology at St. Mary's College in Moraga, California, and is presently professor of theology and scripture at St. Bernard's Institute, Graduate School of Theology and Ministry, in Albany, New York. In his work Church History: Twenty Centuries of Catholic Christianity, *Dwyer examines the history of the Catholic Church from its beginnings to the papacy of John Paul II. In the following excerpt from this work, Dwyer explores and analyzes the historical and traditional aspects of the Jewish life into which Jesus was born and from which the roots of Christianity derive. He maintains that one cannot fully understand the person of Jesus, and therefore the history of the early church, without first comprehending the underlying values, traditions, and conflicts prevalent in Jewish society during that time. He argues, for example, that throughout Jewish history, the messianic prophecies of the Old Testament held out to the Jewish people a time of extraordinary gladness and hope, when God would come and dwell among them. These prophecies found their fulfillment in the person of Jesus Christ, he writes. Dwyer also points out that as a Jew, Jesus was subject to the same laws and traditions that governed Jewish society in his day. However, he asserts that it is these same beliefs and values that Jesus sought to challenge and question.*

Jesus was a Jew, as were all of his earliest followers. They all lived and acted out of a rich tradition which was already over a thousand years old by the time Jesus was born. Jesus' own preaching and the word which others preached about him are unintelligible without an understanding of what it meant to be a Jew during the middle years of the first century of our era.

Jewish History Began with Abraham

First of all, to be a Jew meant to have a history which was intimately connected with the land of Israel. According to Jewish tradition, this history began with Abraham, a nomadic chieftain, who answered the call of God and traveled from a city in Mesopotamia near the Persian Gulf, to the land which would later become Israel. Abraham himself did not become a permanent settler in the land, but wandered about in it, pasturing his flocks, as did his son and grandson after him. According to the same ancient Jewish tradition, Abraham's great-grandson, Joseph, had been sold into slavery in Egypt by his own brothers. There, through a remarkable series of events, he won the favor of the Pharaoh, reached high position, and at a time of famine in Israel, brought his father and brothers to Egypt, where they lived as honored guests. Later with the accession to power of a "Pharaoh who knew not Joseph," their position changed, and they became little better than slaves.

God Intervenes in Human History

According to this tradition, hundreds of years later God appeared to Moses, an Israelite who had been given an Egyptian upbringing, and commissioned him to lead the Israelites out of Egypt and into freedom. After escaping from Pharaoh's forces through the direct intervention of God, Moses and the Israelites wandered in the desert and eventually came to the mountain of Sinai. Here God appeared again to Moses, and through him gave the Israelites the *Law,* a detailed list of the demands which God made on the people he had chosen to be his own. After further wandering, Moses died, and under Joshua, his successor, the Israelites moved into the land which had been promised them, and through a combination of conquest and infiltration claimed the land as their own. Here they lived in a loose confederation, occasionally uniting under charismatic leaders to defend themselves against hostile neighbors. By the middle of the eleventh century B.C. they found themselves subject to increasing pressure from the Philistines, a people recently arrived on the western coast of Palestine. Faced with the Philistine threat, they united somewhat hesitantly, under a king named Saul. This first experiment in monarchy was a failure, but in the year 1000 B.C., David became king of the united monarchy of Israel (in the north) and Judah (in the South) and he, followed by his son, Solomon, ruled the united monarchy, each for about forty years.

After Solomon's death, the kingdom was divided, and the Old Testament tells the story of the next four hundred years as a tale of internal strife within the kingdoms and of their attempts to retain or regain their independence from foreign powers. These attempts finally failed. The northern kingdom lost its independence and its population was dispersed in 721 B.C. Judah fell to Babylon in 597 B.C. and this marked the end of Israelite independence. These developments led, not to despair, but to an ever more intense longing for the restoration of the kingdom of David—a restoration which would be effected by one who, like David and the kings of Judah after him, would be an *Anointed One*, called by God and endowed with the power to fulfill God's will in history. The Hebrew word for "Anointed One" has given us the word *Messiah*. . . .

Important Elements of Jewish History

Jewish faith in Jesus' day (and this includes the faith of all of Jesus' earliest followers) can be understood only against the background of the history of Israel, which has been sketched in the briefest possible compass here. There are a number of elements in this Jewish faith which are extremely important for an understanding of Jesus. *First*, unlike all of the other nations and ethnic groups of their day, the Jews had room for only one God—a God who was absolutely transcendent and therefore infinitely holy, his reality separated from ours by an unbridgeable chasm.

But there is a *second* affirmation of Jewish faith which stands in a paradoxical relationship with the first: this absolutely transcendent God has intervened directly and immediately in history, and has revealed himself in his total control of the historical process, both within Israel and in the world at large. For Israel it was the Exodus from Egypt which was the great revelation of this God who is the lord of history, for it was at that time that "with a mighty hand and outstretched arm" he led a mixed band of slaves out of Egypt, toward the land which he had promised to their forefathers. And although perhaps only a small percentage of the Israelites in David's day actually had ancestors who had been in Egypt, all later Israelites adopted the story of the Exodus as their story and as the revelation of their God. Israel understood itself as the people of this God, on whose behalf he had acted on the stage of world history. For God did not address the Jew solely as an individual, but as a member of a *people*, God's people, who had a past, a present, and a future, precisely because God had definitively intervened in history in their favor.

A *third* element of Jewish faith is the conviction that after leading their ancestors out of Egypt, God made a *covenant* with them (that is, an agreement or contract) in which he formally stated that he would be their God and they would be his people, and in which he laid down the conditions which were binding on them because of this agreement. These conditions were summed up in the *Law*—the clear and detailed statement of God's will for his people. Israel understood this Law not as a burden to be borne grudgingly, but as God's greatest gift, and as a source of peace and of joy.

A *fourth* element in Jewish faith appeared in many variant forms. In the Jewish view, God's plan embraced the entire human race and Israel was destined to play a special role in asserting God's lordship over the whole world. This vision could be narrowly nationalized, and this happened frequently enough, whenever Israel identified its own political or military success with the triumph of the cause of God. But the vision could be broadened, and at least at certain times Israel was conscious of playing a part in God's plan for the entire human race. This element of Jewish faith was an important part of the belief in a *Messiah*—an individual chosen and commissioned by God to liberate Israel and to lead it to the fulfillment of its vocation. . . .

Importance of Jewish History to Christianity

This summary of Jewish faith and life in Jesus' day is minimal, but it is indispensable for the understanding of Jesus. This is true, not because Jesus was totally conditioned by his world and its values, but precisely because he distanced himself from that world and questioned its values, and, above all, its picture of God. But Jesus did this, not by rejecting the God of the Old Testament or the faith for which that God called; he did it by claiming to reveal the one who had been the God of Israel from the beginning, and he did it by reaffirming the faith for which that God had called, but which had been obscured and sometimes lost under a suffocating layer of human religiosity.

Israel's history is important for another reason: the early church saw itself as the new Israel, as the fulfillment of the hope and longing of Israel's prophets and holy men, and as the new and definitive people of God. For this reason, the church's image of itself and the picture which it strove to present to the world are both unintelligible without an understanding of Jewish faith and hope in Jesus' time.

The Role of St. Peter

Stephen K. Ray

Formerly a member of the Baptist church, Stephen K. Ray is a convert to Catholicism. Since his conversion, Ray has been a frequent speaker at conferences and writes for several Catholic magazines. He is the author of Crossing the Tiber, *which describes his conversion to the Catholic faith. In this excerpt from his work* Upon This Rock: St. Peter and the Primacy of Rome in Scripture and the Early Church, *Ray examines the life and ministry of the apostle Peter. Ray notes that in every list of the apostles throughout the New Testament, it is Peter who is placed first. In addition, Ray describes many instances throughout the New Testament in which Peter plays the central role as Jesus' disciple. He argues that the greatest single event that memorializes Peter as one leader of the church is recorded in St. Matthew's Gospel. In this gospel, Christ calls Peter "the rock," a symbol of strength and unity. Ray states that Peter assumed the leading role in the fledgling church after Christ returned to his father in heaven. According to Ray, Peter traveled far and wide throughout the Roman Empire, establishing churches. This Catholic belief that Jesus chose Peter as the first "pope" is known as the Petrine papacy.*

W hy should we consider someone so impulsive, outspoken, and unstable as Peter to be capable of leading the band of apostles in founding and governing the Church, the Household of God? Because he is respected and loved by Jesus, being the first among the closest associates of Jesus. Jesus often separated out Peter, James, and John for intimate times of prayer and special instruction. Jesus also specifically

Stephen K. Ray, "Part One: Biblical Study: Peter the Man, the Apostle, and the Rock," in *Upon This Rock: St. Peter and the Primacy of Rome in Scripture and the Early Church*, San Francisco, CA: Ignatius Press, 1999, pp. 23–62. Copyright © 1999 Ignatius Press, San Francisco. All rights reserved. Reproduced by permission.

chose Peter to be the leader and spokesman for the apostles and the primitive Christian community.

Peter Listed First Among the Apostles

Every list of the twelve apostles in the New Testament has Peter prominently placed at the top of the list, and Judas is listed last. Peter was the first of three special disciples whom Jesus included in his inner circle. Peter is repeatedly mentioned by name when the others are referred to simply as "disciples" or "the eleven". He always stands out as the leader, the spokesman, and the chosen "first" among equals. The names Peter, Simon, or Cephas are used 191 times in the New Testament. Except for Christ himself, no other person receives nearly as much attention as Simon Peter does through biblical references. Before Jesus called this fisherman and renamed him Peter, his name was Simon, son of Jonas. Jesus gave Simon a new, descriptive name, Peter, which means "rock" in Greek, and from that time forward he was known as Simon Peter. Jesus in Caesarea Philippi also called him Cephas (Aramaic for "rock"). As we see from the naming of the twelve sons of Jacob, names were very significant in Jewish society. In the Torah and in Jewish tradition, a name change meant a change in status. Abraham, the father of the Jews who received the covenant sign of circumcision, had his name changed by God from Abram, meaning "father", to Abraham, meaning the "father of nations" (Gen 17:1–5). Now, at the inception of the new covenant, we see Simon's name changed by Jesus from Simon to *Kepha*, Peter, signifying a new designation, a new commission, and a new status. . . .

Peter and John [the Baptist] were not highly educated; in fact, the rulers of the people and elders watched "Peter and John, and perceived that they were uneducated, common men." [Acts 4:13] Peter's brother Andrew, who was a disciple of John the Baptist at the time, introduced Peter to Jesus. Peter owned fishing boats and a family fishing business in partnership with James and John, the sons of Zebedee. It was from Peter's boat that Jesus chose to speak to the multitudes (Lk 5:3). Peter and his brother Andrew, along with James and John, left their everyday life and businesses to follow Jesus as his disciples. What happened to their boats and nets? What happened to their fishing business? We do not know. Maybe the business was carried on by family members, possibly by Zebedee and his hired servants (Mk 1:20). After the Resurrection, Peter and the other disciples were again fishing from a boat in the Sea of Galilee (Jn 21:3), so it is probable that Peter still owned the fishing vessels.

Peter Is First Among Jesus' Disciples

The New Testament is peppered with biographical details about the personality and life of Peter. For three years Peter and the disciples followed Jesus as he crisscrossed the rocky terrain of Israel. Peter walked on the water (Mt 14:28–31) and pulled a coin from a fish's mouth to pay a tax for himself and Jesus (Mt 17:24–27). Peter was the one who received a revelation from God that enabled him to confess the true identity of Jesus (Mt 16:16), and he saw Jesus transfigured, along with Moses and Elijah, on the mountain, which he mentions later in his second epistle. Peter, along with John, was selected to prepare the Passover meal, which would be transformed into the Eucharist (Lk 22:8). Peter was bold and spoke his mind— sometimes too quickly, not thinking before he did so. He was rebuked by Jesus for his wrong-headed conclusions (Mt 16:23), though Jesus loved his devotion and courage. After pledging loyalty and even martyrdom for Jesus' sake, Peter reneged and vehemently denied the Lord three times—and then (unlike Judas) repented and wept bitterly because of his betrayal. Another time, he impulsively drew his sword and slashed off Malchus' ear (Jn 18:10). Even though he was brash and impulsive, however, he had a gentle heart and was extremely sensitive to his sin and shortcomings. . . .

Peter Leads the Church

Peter was the first man to see Jesus after the Resurrection. Peter was given the special commission to pray for his brethren and strengthen them and was appointed by Jesus to feed and tend his sheep. After Pentecost, Peter took the leading role in the fledgling Church. He preached the first gospel message (Acts 2:14–40), and, with the assistance of the other apostles, he baptized over three thousand people that day.

After exposing their deception, Peter condemned Ananias and Sapphira, who lied to the Holy Spirit and fell dead at the feet of Peter (Acts 5:1–22). Peter changed the course of the young Church by baptizing Cornelius and his household, the first Gentiles to become Christians. Paul came to visit Cephas (Peter) and "remained with him fifteen days" (Gal 1:18). Later, Paul again came to Jerusalem to submit his gospel to Peter and the leading apostles to make sure he was not running in vain (Gal 2:2). When confusion arose over how the law of circumcision applied to the Gentile converts, Peter made the authoritative doctrinal decision at the first Church council in Jerusalem (Acts 15), to which all those in attendance acquiesced. Peter traveled extensively, preaching the gospel and establishing churches all over the Roman Empire. There are many more biographical passages focusing on Peter in the Scriptures. . . .

How does Peter fit into the whole scheme of things? Did Jesus really treat Peter differently from the others? Did Jesus favor Peter or set him apart? What about the other disciples? Did they recognize Peter as first, in a place of preeminence? John was the disciple "Jesus loved", the one who rested his head on Jesus' breast while at the Passover dinner, but it was Peter who was given a special place of leadership, the shepherd of the sheep and the one who "strengthens" his fellow apostles. But the single event that most clearly shows Peter's prominence in the New Testament is recorded in the Gospel of St. Matthew. Jesus commissions Peter, and his words have probably caused more spilled ink over the last five centuries than any other biblical passage.

The Gospels, Acts, and the letter to the Galatians give us the most information about the ministry of Peter after the Resurrection. The Acts of the Apostles begins with Peter at the center of activity in Jerusalem; and then, after the Council of Jerusalem, Paul takes center stage in the drama. . . .

As we enter the fascinating period of the apostolic Church, we see that the place of Peter, and his martyrdom in Rome, had a universal acceptance among the writings and beliefs of the earliest Christians.

Peter's Primacy in the Early Church

Now we will plunge into the Scriptures to discover passages related to Peter and his primacy in the early Church, a primacy that was passed on in the Church through the office of the bishop of Rome.

The Gospel of John

—event c. A.D. 30

—written by St. John about A.D. 90–100

"One of the two who heard John speak, and followed him, was Andrew, Simon Peter's brother. He first found his brother Simon, and said to him, 'We have found the Messiah' (which means Christ). He brought him to Jesus. Jesus looked at him, and said, 'So you are Simon the son of John? You shall be called Cephas' (which means Peter)" [Jn 1:40–42].

The Gospel of Matthew

—event c. A.D. 30

—written in the last half of the first century

"The names of the twelve apostles are these: first, Simon, who is called Peter, and Andrew his brother; James the son of Zebedee, and John his brother; Philip and Bartholomew; Thomas and Matthew the tax collector; James the son of Alphaeus, and Thaddaeus; Simon the Cananaean, and Judas Iscariot, who betrayed him" [Mt. 10:2–4]. . . .

Jesus Christ in the Gospel of Matthew

"Now when Jesus came into the district of Caesarea Philippi, he asked his disciples, 'Who do men say that the Son of man is?' And they said, 'Some say John the Baptist, others say Elijah, and others Jeremiah or one of the prophets.' He said to them, 'But who do you say that I am?' Simon Peter replied, 'You are the Christ, the Son of the living God.' And Jesus answered him, 'Blessed are you, Simon Bar-Jona! For flesh and blood has not revealed this to you, but my Father who is in heaven. And I tell you, you are Peter, and on this rock I will build my church, and the powers of death shall not prevail against it. I will give you the keys of the kingdom of heaven, and whatever you bind on earth shall be bound in heaven, and whatever you loose on earth shall be loosed in heaven.' Then he strictly charged the disciples to tell no one that he was the Christ." . . .

Jesus Christ in the Gospel of John
—speaking to Peter after the Resurrection

"'Simon, son of John, do you love me more than these?' He said to him, 'Yes, Lord; you know that I love you.' He said to him, 'Feed my lambs.' A second time he said to him, 'Simon, son of John, do you love me?' He said to him, 'Yes, Lord; you know that I love you.' He said to him, 'Tend my sheep.' He said to him a third time, 'Simon, son of John, do you love me?' Peter was grieved because he said to him the third time, 'Do you love me?' And he said to him, 'Lord, you know everything; you know that I love you.' Jesus said to him, 'Feed my sheep [Jn 21:15–17].'" . . .

Peter Was Entrusted with a Sacred Mission

Since the Protestant Reformation, many have ignored, even attacked the ancient teachings of the Church and have tried to empty the biblical passages of any hierarchical significance. The winds of freedom and democracy that have swept Europe in the past few centuries have not failed to have an impact on biblical study and perceptions of Church government. Too often the Church is perceived as a democracy instead of as a kingdom. Jesus Christ reestablished the eternal throne of David and also reestablished the office of royal steward "over the house" when he chose Peter, investing him with the keys of the kingdom of heaven. Peter may have died, but his office continues, and his successors . . . continue to fill his office of royal steward and continue to preserve the sacred deposit of truth entrusted to the Church by the apostles.

Emperor Constantine's Conversion to Christianity

Hans A. Pohlsander

Hans A. Pohlsander is emeritus professor of classics and religious studies at the State University of New York at Albany and is the author of Helena: Empress and Saint. *According to Pohlsander, the rise of Constantine to power as the new leader of the Roman Empire in 312 had enormous implications for the fledging Christian Church. In his work* Emperor Constantine, *excerpted below, Pohlsander states that Constantine's first act as emperor was to restore the rights of Christians to practice their religion, thereby putting an end to the persecution of Christians in his territories. Despite this act of tolerance, Pohlsander maintains, Constantine did not at first fully embrace Christianity. Coins minted in his honor, for example, still displayed images of the ancient gods Mars and Apollo.*

According to Pohlsander, before the crucial battle of Milvian Bridge in the year 312, between the Roman emperors Constantine the Great and Maxentius over control of the Roman Empire, Constantine had a dream in which God commanded him to use the sign of Christ on the shields of his soldiers. Constantine carried out these instructions and was victorious in battle. According to ancient sources, Pohlsander writes, Constantine henceforth became a believer in the power of the Christian god.

Constantine's conversion had a great impact on the development of Christianity. Pohlsander notes that as a result of the emperor's adherence to Christianity, the church and the state were no longer separate and distinct. Not only did Constantine believe he was appointed by God to rule the world, he also regarded himself as a "common bishop" who actively sought to im-

Hans A. Pohlsander, "Constantine's Conversion," in *The Emperor Constantine*. Andover, Hampshire, UK: Routledge, 1996, pp. 21–28. Copyright © 1996 Hans A. Pohlsander. Reproduced by permission of Taylor & Francis Books UK.

pose on the church his own imperialistic designs. At the same time, Pohlsander notes that from 312 to 320 Constantine retained the high priest title of Pontifex Maximus, *in deference to his subjects, who were mainly pagan.*

Constantine ended all persecution in his territories as soon as he came to power, providing not only for toleration but also for restitution. He acted formally and on his own, without consulting his imperial colleagues. He was not, however, at this time ready to embrace Christianity himself. His coinage evidences devotion first to Mars and then increasingly to Apollo, reverenced as *Sol Invictus,* "the unconquered sun." A panegyrist who addressed Constantine at Trier in 310, after the swift action against Maximian [appointed Caesar 285], will have us believe that Constantine, on his way back from Massilia visited "the world's most" beautiful temple, probably meaning the shrine of Apollo Grannus at Grand (near Neufchâtel, Vosges), and there experienced a vision: Apollo, accompanied by Victory, appeared to him and presented him with (four?) laurel crowns, promising a long and prosperous reign. The panegyrist's fulsome flattery continues: Constantine is the one whose coming "the divine songs of poets have prophesied." Significant is also that henceforth Constantine dissociates himself from the Herculians, the party of [Emperor] Maxentius; the new propaganda line claims that Constantine's father Constantius was a descendant of the emperor Claudius Gothicus (268–70); although the specific relationship was not made clear. Again the dynastic principle prevailed over the tetrarchic principle.

Constantine's Dream

The next significant step in Constantine's religious development occurred in 312. [Christian scholar] Lactanius reports that during the night before the Battle of the Milvian Bridge Constantine was commanded in a dream to place the sign of Christ on the shields of his soldiers. The sign, it is widely believed, was the Chi-Rho, X, although Lactantius language on this point is not very clear. (Chi, X, and Rho, P, are the first two letters of the Greek form of "Christ;" in the monogram the two letters are written in ligature.) Constantine did as he had been told—his overwhelmingly pagan troops must have been puzzled—won the battle and from then on believed in the power of "the God of the Christians."

Twenty-five years later [Bishop] Eusebius, in his *Life of Constantine*, gives us a far different account, one which Constantine himself had given to Eusebius, and under oath: When Constantine and the army were on their march toward Rome—neither the time nor the place is specified—they observed in broad daylight a strange phenomenon in the sky: a cross of light and the words "by this sign you will be victor." During the next night Christ appeared to Constantine and instructed him to place the heavenly sign on the battle standards of his army. The new battle standard became known as the *labarum*.

The two accounts are difficult to reconcile. Of the two, that by Lactantius is by far the more believable. Eusebius' account, while it fits the religious environment of his times, is suspect on account of both its timing and its substance. If the phenomenon was observed by the entire army, why then was it not more widely known? The phenomenon, if it did indeed appear, may have been a solar halo. Some scholars think that the *labarum* was not in use before 324. . . .

Constantine Professes Christianity

We may be certain that in 312, before or during the battle, Constantine had an experience of some sort which was probably interpreted for him by Bishop Ossius (or Hosius) of Cordoba, who accompanied him, and which demonstrated to him the power of "the God of Christians" and prompted him to profess Christianity. We may also be certain that this was more a matter of religious conviction than a matter of politi-

cal expediency. Constantine was not a freethinker but a believer; he apparently had a deeply-felt need to place himself
under the protection of a supreme deity. Professing Christianity gave him no advantage that could not be obtained by mere
toleration, and the Christians were still very much a minority,
especially in the West. Not too long after the capture of Rome,
Constantine sent to the bishop of Carthage and to the pro-
consul of Africa letters which leave no doubt that he favored
the Christian religion, subsidized the Christian church from
public funds, exempted the clergy from public obligations, believed the proper worship of "the Deity" to be of vital importance for the welfare of the empire, and regarded himself as
God's servant. But in what sense he became a Christian and
how well he understood the Christian message is another
question.

Late in 311 or early in 312 . . . but before the Battle of the
Milvian Bridge, Constantine betrothed his half-sister Constantia (one of the six children of Constantius and Theodora) to
his fellow-emperor Licinius. Constantia was then eighteen
years old at most, while Licinius was more than twice her
age. . . .

Toleration for the Christians

Probably in February 313, the two emperors had met in Milan. On this occasion the marriage of Constantia to Licinius
took place. (It would be interesting to know by what rites this
marriage was celebrated or how Constantia felt about this
match.) At Milan, too, the two emperors agreed on a common
religious policy. The agreement found expression, several
months later, in the edict which is commonly but erroneously
called the Edict of Milan. The text of this edict is recorded in
Latin by Lactantius and in Greek by Eusebius. It is actually a
letter addressed by Licinius to the governors of the provinces
formerly controlled by Maximinus Daia. It instructs the re-
cipients that all persecution of Christians is to cease, that con-

fiscated Christian property, whether individual or corporate, is to be speedily restored and that all citizens, Christians specifically but also all others, are to be free to practise whatever religion they choose. It granted the religious toleration for which the Christian apologists had pleaded in the past. It did not alter the status of Christians in the West. It extended to Christians in the East the same protection which Christians in the West already enjoyed. It did not establish Christianity as a state religion; it did not commit Licinius personally to the Christian faith.

To return now to Constantine. There is no doubt that he was sympathetic to the Christians already before 312, that in 312 he committed himself personally to the Christian faith, and that in time his commitment to and understanding of that faith deepened. At the same time he seems to have realized that most of his subjects and especially the senatorial nobility in Rome were pagan, and he avoided offering offence to them. He still held the office of *pontifex maximus*. Christian symbols are slow to appear on his coins. The famous triumphal arch erected in his honor by the senate and completed in 315 is another case in point. There are no Christian symbols on the arch, and its language is religiously neutral: Constantine, it says, gained victory over the "tyrant" (Maxentius) "by the prompting of the Divinity (*instinctu divinitatis*) and by the greatness of his mind (*magnitudine mentis*)." He is the "liberator of the city" and the "establisher of peace."

It is now generally accepted that Constantine did not receive baptism until shortly before his death. It would be a mistake to interpret this as a lack of sincerity or commitment. In the fourth and fifth centuries Christians often delayed their baptism until late in life. This was true not only of Constantine but also of Constantius II, Theodosius I, and even St. Ambrose. St Augustine comments on it in his *Confessions*. The practice was not, however, encouraged by the church....

Constantine Oversees the Church

We must turn our attention once more to the events of 312, to the decision which Constantine made in that year about religion. That decision, far from being a private matter, and its implementation within the remaining twenty-five years of Constantine's life, profoundly affected both church and state, religion and politics in the Roman world. Religion and politics were, of course, closely intertwined in the Roman world, just as they had been in the Greek world. Changes in one would inevitably bring changes in the other.

In the nearly three hundred years of its previous existence the church had periodically been subject to persecution; at the same time it had enjoyed independence. By his active involvement in its affairs, however benevolent, Constantine deprived the church of that independence. He deemed himself not only a divinely appointed ruler of the world but also a *koinos episkopos* (common bishop), that is, a general overseer and arbiter of church affairs. He used the church as an instrument of imperial policy and imposed upon it his imperial ideology. His desire for harmony and unity in the church took precedence over all other considerations. Clearly the church was now obliged to adopt a different attitude toward the empire, towards government authority, and toward military service. When the bishops assumed some judicial and administrative functions the church not only endorsed but became part of the apparatus of government.

The first Christians had been a humble and downtrodden minority. With the passing of time that gradually changed and Christians increasingly could be found among the urban middle class. By [Emperor] Diocletian's time we encounter them even at the court and elsewhere in imperial service, both civilian and military. But only under Constantine did the church acquire power and wealth. The original indifference towards worldly goods now gave way to the use of worldly goods in the service of the church. A decline in spirituality accompanied the process, and the rise of monasticism was, at least in part, a response to that decline and the increasing worldliness of the church.

The Church During the Middle Ages

H.W. Crocker III

H.W. Crocker III is a convert to Catholicism and has worked as a journalist, a speechwriter, and a book editor. He has written several books, including Triumph: The Power and the Glory of the Catholic Church, *which describes the two-thousand-year history of the Catholic Church. In the following excerpt from this book, Crocker discusses the alliance between medieval warrior kings and the church during the Middle Ages in Europe. This affiliation safeguarded the church against invading marauders, Crocker asserts, but inevitably destabilized it.*

Crocker states that under their warrior kings, Frankish knights helped thwart the spread of Islam in 710 and 732, thereby preserving the Christian kingdom from the forces of Islam. He maintains that the most formidable of all the warrior kings was Charlemagne, known also as Charles the Great, or Carolus Magnus. Born in 742, Charlemagne was a brilliant military strategist who conducted approximately fifty military campaigns throughout western Europe. His goal was to convert all those he captured to the Christian faith. On Christmas Day in the year 800, the pope crowned Charlemagne the emperor of the West. Crocker argues that after Charlemagne's death, the alliance between the church and the warrior kings became problematic. Lacking Charlemagne's innate military abilities, his successors were unsuccessful in defeating their enemies. Consequently, marauding Vikings terrorized and pillaged churches and murdered priests and monks. Moreover, Islamic forces sought to conquer the West and claim its territories for the Muslim faith. Many years of warfare followed, with the church constantly under siege. However, in the tenth century the German king, Otto the Great (936–973), finally restored the greatness of the Holy Roman Empire.

The kings of the early Middle Ages might not have been philosopher-kings like Marcus Aurelius. Many of them, like Charlemagne, were not even literate. By the standards of the Church they could be seen, accurately, as bloodstained fornicators. But their hearts were in the right place. One can usefully think of them as rather like the motorcyclists who descend on Washington, D.C., every Memorial Day waving American and MIA flags. Only the "Bikers for the Bishop of Rome" would be waving the papal flag or the white flag with the crimson cross of the Crusades. The best of them would be staffing monasteries, designing cathedrals, and creating the cultural tapestry of the Middle Ages. To put it as a cynic might, the newly converted barbarians of the West exhibited a nobler, humbler, less refined savagery than the Oriental despots of Byzantium. They were also commendably loyal to Rome. . . .

The heroes of this story are the noble Franks, a Germano-Belgic tribe. It was from their blood that sprang Clovis, founder of the alliance between the Franks and the Church at the end of the fifth century with his crowning in Reims Cathedral, which would be the holy site of consecration for French monarchs for nearly thirteen hundred years. It was Frankish knights under their warrior-kings who fought the early battles against the Moors, thwarting the rising tide of Islam that came sweeping up the Iberian Peninsula in 710.

Clovis was of the Merovingian line, but the royal mantle would eventually be borne by the Carolingians, who descended from Charles Martel, the hammer that halted the Moors at the battle of Poitiers in 732. That victory preserved the Franks' Catholic kingdom from what had befallen the Visigoths in what was now Saracen Spain. Charles's son Pepin III—also known as Pepin the Short—was the first king in the Carolingian dynasty, crowned by the pope's representative, a British monk, St. Boniface. Pope Stephen II (752–757) strengthened the bond between the Franks and the Church by affirming Pepin's line as the only royal house of the Franks. He consecrated them as the pope's defenders against the barbarian Lombards and tyrannical Byzantines. Pepin drove the Lombards from northern and central Italy in two campaigns, in 754 and 756, making a gift of his latter conquests to the pope, thus creating the Papal States: a swath of territory that would be ruled directly from the Vatican for eleven hundred years.

Charlemagne

But the greatest of Carolingian kings was Pepin's son, Charlemagne, who in 774 not only conquered the Lombards—adding them to the Frankish kingdom—but deftly captured every rival claimant to the Frankish throne. A strong, handsome, and vigorous military prince, he had all the barbarian virtues, an army and imperial policy unmatched since the days of the Roman legions, and a sword consecrated to the Church. It is estimated that he fought more than fifty campaigns from one end of Western Europe to the other, often with the express goal of defeating and converting heathen tribes who would as soon burn a missionary as listen to the gospel. Charlemagne waged campaigns to the east against the Avars, to the north against the Saxons and the Vikings, and to the south across the Pyrenees against the Moors, a campaign that would later be immortalized in *The Song of Roland*. His Frankish armies fought throughout Italy, southern Germany, and the islands of the Mediterranean. His goal was that of all warrior-kings—conquest—but also conversion of the conquered to the Catholic faith.

Papal elections were going through a turbulent period, and Charlemagne brought his sword to bear here as well. The constant trouble was that factions formed around potential candidates and elections could be disrupted, or reversed, as mobs and troops intervened on behalf of their favorite. Even after a pope was elected unanimously by the clerics of Rome—as in the case of Pope Leo III (795–816)—he could find himself under physical attack by his enemies. Leo was dragged from his horse and beaten nearly to death by partisan thugs who attempted to tear out his eyes and his tongue, though both his sight and his speech recovered—miraculously, it is said—from the damage of their brutal fingers. Leo turned to Charlemagne for protection, and he got it. In return, Pope Leo III crowned Charlemagne emperor of the West on Christmas Day 800 and became the only pope in history to kneel before a king. It was Pope Leo III who also—against his better judgment—allowed Charlemagne to install the *filioque* in the creed, affirming that the Holy Spirit came from the Father *and from the Son*. Theologically it was sound, but the pope objected not to its theology, but to *any* change on principle, as he was bound to do by Rome's traditional conservatism, especially change recommended by a layman. But Charlemagne, who took the Christian aspects of his empire seriously—his crowning marks the beginning of the Holy Roman Empire—thought from his own experience in the provinces that the *filioque* was essential to explaining the true faith to the Western tribes, and the pope reluctantly complied.

The Collaboration Between Charlemagne and the Pope

Charlemagne also encouraged the pope as a secular ruler. It was at Charlemagne's insistence that the pope maintained his own war fleet to protect himself from Saracen raiding parties. The Moors had by this time transformed much of the Mediterranean into an Islamic lake. The pope thus became, in defense, not only the Vicar of Christ and Lord Temporal of the Papal States but First Sea Lord of the Vatican.

It should also be mentioned that the Church assisted in the secular rule of Charlemagne's dominions. Beneath the emperor was a feudal network of nobles, as well as an occasional parliament made up of both lords and bishops, who governed in tandem. In Charlemagne's kingdom, the crozier of Christ's shepherds and the scepter of the king were united in governing a Christian people of many tribes and languages, but one Catholic faith.

Though illiterate, Charlemagne was nevertheless an educated man within an oral tradition, being able to understand Greek and Latin (which he could also speak), as well as his own Germanic tongue. As a sort of retirement hobby, he even tried to teach himself to write. He was consumed by a desire to learn and was interested in every academic subject. He eagerly followed theological debates and listened to readings from the Church fathers, his preference being for St. Augustine's *City of God*, which, in his position, had obvious practical applications. He was a great patron of learning, the arts, and religion, founding schools that became the foundations of Western Europe's first universities. He established institutes for church music, required the Church to provide a classical education for its clergy, and protected clerical privileges while insisting on clerical discipline. In addition, he promoted scholarship and encouraged writers to record Frankish legends, history, and law. Charlemagne's devotion to the work of monks and scholars in copying classical manuscripts ensured that these books survived beyond the Dark Ages. Among the scholars advanced by Charlemagne were Einhard, who became his biographer, and Alcuin of York, who revised St. Jerome's Vulgate Bible.

Charlemagne's Religious Empire

Charlemagne was a political and military genius, the savior of learning in the West, and the founder of the ideal and the reality of Western Europe as an entity united by Frankish swords and Catholic dogma. His Catholic empire stretched from France in the west to his military outposts on the borderlands of the Slavs and Byzantines. Given that so many missionaries came from Britain during this period—fulfilling Pope St. Gregory the Great's dream—one can even include the British Isles as a cultural and religious ally of Charlemagne. To the north, Frankish dominion extended over Germany, which he shielded from the Vikings. To the south it went all the way to the Pyrenees, where his knights confronted the rival Islamic empire.

Charlemagne as a man was as big as his domains, a towering six-foot-four Aryan hero, popular, intelligent in his tastes, moderate at his table, and of dynamic energy. He had four wives (in succession), numerous mistresses, eighteen children (eight of whom were legitimate), and a love of home life so strong that he forbade his daughters to marry. Rather than be deprived of their company, he winked at their illicit affairs, just as the Church agreed to wink at his own royal liaisons. Time, unfortunately, advances, and those of us separated from Charlemagne by more than a millennium can only sigh for those days when one could be both a Catholic warrior and a Frankish barbarian without contradiction. . . .

The Church Becomes a Target

But Charlemagne's successors lacked the great man's gift for defeating calamities. His Carolingian successors fell into dynastic wars and disputes—especially after the death of Louis the Pious, whose sons were Adams of rebellion and who himself died while campaigning to settle such a war. It was the Church, then, that proved the most effective and reliable administrator of the West, and it was the Church that began to overshadow the crown, or, rather, the numerous crowns, as the West divided itself into a series of smaller kingdoms. The West was the Church. The various kings represented the Church—in arms, and arms the Church needed in plenty.

Churchmen were now the prime targets of the greatest outlaw tribe of the West, the Vikings, whose vast and frequent raiding parties were a source of terror from Ireland to Russia. They were an especial terror to the Church, because the Vikings saw churches and monasteries as easily plunderable treasure chests of golden goblets and jewel-encrusted crucifixes. To unfortunate cities like Tours, Viking invasions represented unpredictable, but periodic, plagues of fire, sword, rape, and pillage.

While Viking raids were unleashed like lightning from the north, Islamic scimitars surged like flames from the south, attacking Rome, capturing the islands of the Mediterranean, and seizing the Moor-facing coast of France. If the Vikings represented sheer brigandage, the Saracens of the Sahara were something else—not only a military but a religious challenge that intended to turn the Western world east to the God of the Prophet Mohammed.

In these wars, it was, again, bishops and abbots who defended the battlements of the Western world, directing armies and often living and falling by the sword. Catholic belief brings the assurance that disasters, too, will pass; and they do. For what was the fate of the fierce Norsemen? Those who eventually settled in Normandy mockingly paid homage to the king of France. Perhaps just as scoffingly they accepted baptism into the Catholic Church. But the faith took hold. The Normans would become another army supporting the Catholic civilization of Europe against the Saracens and the Byzantines.

In the short term, though, things looked bleak. Western Europe was in a perpetual state of warfare and the Church in a perpetual state of siege, with appended monasteries and churches lopped off here and there, sacked and destroyed, their priests, monks, and nuns murdered by any variety of villains. In *la belle France* [beautiful France] recovery began with a new royal house—the house that would govern France for eight hundred years—when the Archbishop of Reims chose Hugh Capet as king in 987.

Restoration of the Holy See

In Germany—seat of the Holy Roman Empire—restoration began with Otto the Great, German king from 936 to 973. In this time of violent upheaval, Otto insisted on reunifying as much of the Holy Roman Empire as possible, leading to warfare against dissident noblemen and conflict with the rival Franks, who were now, to all practical purposes, French in their allegiance rather than German. Otto proved his bravery by trying to restore order in Italy, which had fallen into a state of moral and political chaos from which it has never fully recovered.

Though France would go its own way, and Italy could not be saved, Otto made two crucial contributions to Europe. He defeated the [Hungarians] Magyars—shutting them up into Hungary—and he restored Charlemagne's dream of an empire where Church and state were united in providing stability and justice. While Otto's relationship with the papacy was one of eventual conqueror—for its own good, it must be added—he was an enormous benefactor to the Catholic Church in Germany. He defended it from the Magyar hordes, granting it huge territories as ecclesiastical property. Under his sword, missionaries were free to go east, commerce could be conducted, and civilization could be restored. Otto also brought a semblance of order to Rome that would help rescue the See of St. Peter from some of its most inglorious days.

The Contributions of the Monastic Orders

Charles De Montalembert

Monasticism has its roots in the early church of the fourth century. At this time, a group of Christian worshippers called the Desert Fathers and Mothers retreated to the solitude of the desert of Palestine in the Middle East, where they lived in communities and spent their time in prayer, meditation, and study. This movement gave rise to the tradition of monasticism within the church that would expand over the centuries to become the vanguard of the Catholic faith. Writing in the eighteenth century, Charles De Montalembert argues in The Monks of the West: From St. Benedict to St. Bernard, *excerpted below, that although Christian monasticism has been celebrated for its grand accomplishments in science, literature, literary and historical preservation, and the cultivation of lands, these endeavors were secondary to monasticism's central purpose: the attainment of spiritual perfection and moral virtue through acts of "chastity, sacrifice, obedience, and humility."*

Montalembert states that throughout the centuries, the church has flourished and prospered in direct proportion to the sanctity and fervor of its religious orders. This is evidenced, Montalembert maintains, even at the beginning of Christianity, when the monks of Thebaide and Palestine converted many to the faith, despite the tyrannous rule of pagan kings. Montalembert asserts that as bulwarks of Christian civilization, the influence of monastic and religious orders in the church as well as on civil society in the following centuries was unparalleled. In the seventh to ninth centuries, for example, the order of Benedictine monks was instrumental in converting Belgium, England, Ger-

Charles De Montalembert, "Fundamental Character of Monastic Institutions," in *The Monks of the West: From St. Benedict to St. Bernard*, vol. 1. New York: P.J. Kenedy & Sons, 1912, pp. 5–11.

many, and Scandinavia to the Christian faith. Similarly, new religious orders established by St. Francis and St. Dominic helped renew the church in the thirteenth and fourteenth centuries. In the sixteenth century, the Jesuits, founded by St. Ignatius of Loyola in 1534, helped restore the vitality of the Catholic faith as the Protestant Reformation swept through Europe.

Montalembert was born in London in 1810 to an émigré French nobleman serving in the British Army and was raised largely by his English grandfather. Throughout his life Montalembert championed the relinquishing of power by the state, especially in the arena of religion and beliefs. He was a member of the French Academy, the preeminent French learned body on matters pertaining to the French language.

Some years ago, who understood what a monk really was? For myself, I had no doubt on the subject when I commenced this work. I believed that I know something which approached to the idea of a saint—to that of the Church; but I had not the least notion of what a monk might be, or of the monastic order. I was like my time. In all the course of my education, domestic or public, no one, not even among those who were specially charged to teach me religion and history, no one considered it necessary to give me the least conception of the religious orders. . . . Have not we all come forth from college knowing by heart the list of the mistresses of Jupiter, but ignorant even of the names of the founders of those religious orders which have civilized Europe, and so often saved the Church? . . .

We may, besides, without excess of ambition, claim for the monk a justice more complete than that which he has yet obtained, even from the greater number of the Christian apologists of recent times. In taking up the defence of the religious orders, these writers have seemed to demand grace for those august institutions in the name of the services which they have rendered to the sciences, to letters, and to agriculture. This is to boast the incidental at the expense of the essential. We are doubtless obliged to acknowledge and admire the cultivation of so many forests and deserts, the transcription and preservation of so many literary and historical monuments, and that monastic erudition which we know nothing to replace; these are great services rendered to humanity, which ought, if humanity were just, to shelter the monks under a celestial shield. But there is, besides, something far more worthy of admiration and gratitude—the permanent strife of moral freedom against the bondage of the flesh; the constant effort of a consecrated will in the pursuit and conquest of Christian virtue; the victorious flight of the soul into those supreme regions where she finds again her true, her immortal grandeur. Institutions simply human, powers merely temporal, might perhaps confer upon society the same temporal benefits: that which human powers cannot do, that which they have never undertaken, and in which they never could succeed, is to discipline the soul, to transform it by chastity, by obedience, by sacrifice and humility: to recreate the man wasted by sin into such virtue, that the prodigies of evangelical perfection have become, during long centuries, the daily history of the Church. It is in this that we see the design of the monks, and what they have done. Among so many founders and legislators of the religious life, not one has dreamt of assigning the cultivation of the soil, the copying of manuscripts, the progress of arts and letters, the preservation of historical monuments, as a special aim to his disciples. These offices have been only accessory—the consequence, often indirect and involuntary, of an institution which had in view nothing but the education of the human soul, its conformity to the law of Christ, and the expiation of its native guilt by a life of sacrifice and mortification. This was for all of them the end and the beginning, the supreme object of existence, the unique ambition, the sole merit, and the sovereign victory. . . .

Religious Orders: Bulwark of the Catholic Church

Since the end of the Roman persecution, the grandeur, the liberty, and the prosperity of the Church have always been exactly proportioned to the power, the regularity, and the sanctity of the religious orders which she embraces within her bosom. We can affirm it without fear. Everywhere and always she has flourished most when her religious communities have been most numerous, most fervent, and most free.

To the period immediately following the peace of the Church, the monks of the Thebaide and of Palestine, of Lerins and of Marmoutier, secured innumerable champions of orthodoxy against the tyrannous Arians of the Lower Empire. In proportion as the Franks achieved the conquest of Gaul [modern-day France], and became the preponderating race amongst all the Germanic races, they permitted themselves to be influenced, converted, and directed by the sons of St. Benedict and of St. Columba.

From the seventh to the ninth century, it was the Benedictines who gave to the Church, Belgium, England, Germany, and Scandinavia, and who furnished, to the founders of all the kingdoms of the West, auxiliaries indispensable to the establishment of a Christian civilization.

In the tenth and eleventh centuries, the same Benedictines, concentrated under the strong direction of the order of Cluny, contended victoriously against the dangers and abuses of the feudal system, and gave to St. Gregory VII. the army which he needed to save the independence of the Church, to destroy the concubinage of the priests, simony, and the secular occupation of ecclesiastical benefices.

In the twelfth century, the order of Citeaux, crowned by St. Bernard with unrivalled splendor, became the principal instrument of the beneficent supremacy of the Holy See, served as an asylum to St. Thomas of Canterbury, and as a bulwark to the liberty of the Church, till the time of [Pope] Boniface VIII.

New Religious Orders Propagate the Faith

In the thirteenth and fourteenth centuries, the new orders instituted by St. Francis, St. Dominic, and their emulators, maintained and propagated the faith among the souls of men and the social institutions throughout the empire; renewed the contest against the venom of heresy, and against the corruption of morals; substituted for the crusades the work of redeeming Christian captives; and produced, in St. Thomas Aquinas, the prince of Christian doctors and moralists, whom faith consults as the most faithful interpreter of Catholic tradition, and in whom reason recognizes the glorious rival of Aristotle and [french philosopher Rene] Descartes.

In the fifteenth century, the Church underwent the great schism,[1] and all the scandals which resulted from it. The ancient orders, also, had lost their primitive fervor, and no new institution came to renew the vigor of the Christian blood.

And we know what was, in the sixteenth century, the invincible progress of Reform [the Protestant Reformation] until the day when the Jesuits, solemnly approved by the last General Council, came forward to intercept the torrent, and preserve to the Church at least the half of her inheritance.

In the seventeenth century, the splendors of Catholic eloquence and science are contemporary with the great reforms of St. Maux and of La Trappe, with the foundations of St. Francis de Sales and St. Vincent de Paul, and with the marvellous blossoming of Christian charity in all these congregations of women, most part of which survive for our happiness.

Finally, in the eighteenth century, the religious orders ... infected by the corruptions which were engendered by the encroachments of the temporal power, or decimated by persecution, succumbed almost entirely, but at the same time the

---

1. The East-West Schism, often called the "Great Schism," divided the Church into Western Catholicism and Eastern Orthodoxy in 1054.

Church sustained the most humiliating trials, and the world has never been able to believe her nearer to her fall. . . .

God's Stalwart Warriors

We would not confound institutions holy and salutary, but subject to all human infirmities, with the sole institution founded by God and for eternity. We do not deny that the Church may subsist and triumph without them. But up to the present time it has pleased God to establish a glorious conjunction between the prosperity of the Church and that of the religious orders—between their liberty and hers. During ten centuries these orders have been the surest bulwark of the Church, and have supplied her most illustrious pontiffs. During ten centuries the secular clergy, naturally too much exposed to the influences of the world, have almost always been surpassed in devotion, in sanctity, and in courage, by the regulars, withdrawn within their monasteries as within citadels, where they have regained peace and strength in rebaptizing themselves in austerity, discipline, and silence. During ten centuries the Religious have been, as they still are in our own day, the most intrepid missionaries, the most indefatigable propagators of the Gospel. And, in brief, during ten centuries, the religious orders have endowed the Church at the same time with an army active and permanent and with a trustworthy reserve. Like the different forces of the same army, they have displayed, even in the diversity of their rules and tendencies, that variety in unity which constitutes the fruitful loveliness and sovereign majesty of Catholicism; and, beyond this, have practised, as far as consists with human weakness, those evangelical precepts, the accomplishment of which conducts to Christian perfection. Occupied, above all, in opening to themselves the way to heaven, they have given to the world the grandest and most noble of lessons, in demonstrating how high a man can attain upon the wings of love purified by sacrifice, and of enthusiasm regulated by faith.

CHAPTER 2

The Evolution of
the Church

50

The Spanish Inquisition

Henry Kamen

Throughout history, the issue of heresy was problematic for the Catholic church. According to historians, it was often left to the local bishops to deal with those accused of such "crimes." Beginning in the twelfth century, however, Pope Gregory IV officially established what was called the "Inquisition." The courts of the Inquisition, created specifically to deal with heresy, were ecclesiastical courts under the jurisdiction of the church. According to the decree issued by Pope Gregory IV in 1231, individuals accused of crimes of heresy were sent to prison, and their lands and goods were confiscated. Those who confessed to heresy and repented were forgiven and taken back into the fold; those who persisted in their activities were burned at the stake. Led by Dominican monks, the inquisitors were first sent to southern France. By the end of the twelfth century, the Inquisition was firmly established in most of southern Europe.

Accusations of heresy were also directed at Jews and Muslims. This was particularly evident in the Spanish Inquisition. Established in 1480, the Spanish Inquisition, unlike other church tribunals, was governed by a secular court, funded and administered by the Spanish Crown through a central council.

In a revised edition of his original 1965 book The Spanish Inquisition: A Historical Revision *Henry Kamen provides an analysis of the Spanish Inquisition. In the following excerpt from his work, Kamen writes that the Spanish Inquisition sought to interrogate newly converted Jews to the Christian faith ("conversos") in order to establish their involvement in supposed secret Jewish practices. Kamen suggests that the Spanish Inquisition had less to do with religious concerns than with racial bias against people of the Jewish faith. He maintains that attacks against the Jews derived from societal and political pressure to curb the Jewish threat to Spanish society. The Inquisition thus gave legitimacy to anti-Semitic prejudices in Spanish society. It is ironic, Kamen claims, that despite many accusations, there was often very little substantial evidence provided at trials that conversos were involved in secret Jewish practices. The Spanish Inquisition finally came to an end in 1808, with the French occupation of the peninsula.*

Catholic leaders have since viewed the Inquisition as one of the darkest periods in the history of the church. In 2000, at the Day of Pardon Mass in St. Peter's Basilica in the Vatican, Pope Paul II asked for forgiveness for the church's role in "violence that some have committed in service of the truth." The pope's apology references, among other misdeeds, the treatment suffered by heretics at the hands of Inquisitors.

The Spanish Inquisition was established everywhere in Spain several years before the final decision to expel the Jews. In those twelve terrible years, conversos [Jews to Christianity newly converted] and Jews alike suffered from the rising tide of antisemitism. While the latter were being harassed and then threatened with expulsion from dioceses in Aragon and Andalusia, the former were being purged of those who retained vestiges of their ancestral Judaism. Many conversos fled abroad without necessarily intending thereby to defect from the Catholic faith. Refugees feature prominently among those condemned in the early years. In the first two years of the tribunal at Ciudad Real [1492], fifty-two accused were burnt alive but 220 were condemned to death in their absence. In the Barcelona auto de fe of 10 June 1491, three persons were burnt alive but 139 were judged in their absence. In Mallorca the same process was repeated when at the auto of 11 May 1493 only three accused were burnt in person but there were forty-seven burnings of the effigies of absent fugitives.

The figures indicate clearly who bore the brunt of the Inquisition: 99.3 per cent of those tried by the Barcelona tribunal between 1488 and 1505, and 91.6 per cent of those tried by that of Valencia between 1484 and 1530, were conversos of Jewish origin. The tribunal, in other words, was not concerned with heresy in general. It was concerned with only one form of religious deviance: the apparently secret practice of Jewish rites.

Edict of Grace

Information about such practices was gleaned through the edict of grace, which was a procedure modelled on that of the mediaeval Inquisition. The inquisitors would preach a sermon in the district they were visiting, recite a list of heresies, and invite those who wished to discharge their consciences to come forward and denounce themselves or others. If they came forward within the 'period of grace'—usually thirty to forty days—they would be absolved and 'reconciled' to the Church without suffering serious penalties. The benign terms encouraged self-denunciation. The edicts of grace, more than any other factor, served to convince the inquisitors that a heresy problem existed. Before that period, there had been only polemics and rumours. Now the confessions, as [historian] Andrés Bernáldez was later to argue, demonstrated that 'all of them were Jews'.

Hundreds of conversos, well aware that they had at some time been lax in observing the rules of their faith, came forward to admit their offences and be reconciled. In Seville the prisons were filled to overflowing with conversos waiting to be interrogated as a result of their voluntary confessions. In Mallorca 300 persons formed a procession during the first ceremony of contrition in 1488. The tribunal at Toledo initiated its career by reconciling an astonishing total of 2,400 repentant conversos during the year 1486. This is no way implied (despite a common but mistaken assumption) that they were judaizers or had tendencies to Judaism. Fear alone was the spur. Faced by the activity of the inquisitors, who now identified as heresy what many converso Christians had accepted as normal practice within the framework of belief, they felt that it was safer to clear their record. There were very many others who did not trust the Inquisition and preferred flight. They wandered from one province to another, always one step ahead of the reverend fathers. The majority, it seems, preferred to take the risk. They confessed and put themselves in the hands of the inquisitors.

By its willingness to condone the confessions of those who came forward during periods of grace, the Inquisition was accepting that an offence had been committed but that no intended or hidden heresy was involved. Those who confessed and accepted the conditions of penitence were hence forward free of possible civil disabilities. This optimistic view was obviously not accepted by the conversos, who had been forced into a compromising position that, in the long run, brought them further miseries. . . .

Loss of Private Property

Punishment by the Inquisition brought with it a number of civil disabilities. In principle this situation could be avoided. From an early period many who admitted their faults during an edict of grace were allowed to wipe the slate clean by making a cash payment to the inquisitors. It was a welcome source of income to the Holy Office. 'Rehabilitation' by this means must have appeared to many conversos a worthwhile price to pay for security. A major advantage was that no confiscation of goods was exacted of those who confessed voluntarily. Thousands were 'reconciled' to the Catholic faith, in Toledo alone some four thousand three hundred persons in 1486–7. Though there is no evidence of how common it was to rehabilitate offenders, lists that survive from Toledo, Segovia, and several Andalusian towns, show that the inquisitors were quite happy to exact the cash payment from thousands of conversos. There was, of course, no proof that those who paid for 'rehabilitation' were in fact convinced judaizers. Moreover—and this was the sting in the tail of voluntary disclosure—it was a calculated risk whether the inquisitors would accept the repentance implied in confessions. Several were subsequently brought to trial for offences committed after their rehabilitation.

Persecution of Conversos

The determination of the tribunal to strike hard at supposed heresy was unmistakable. Because documentation for the early years has not usually survived, it is difficult to arrive at reliable figures for the activity of the Inquisition. The period of most intense persecution of conversos was between 1480 and 1530. Hernando del Pulgar [a historian of the era] estimated that up to 1490 the Inquisition in Spain had burnt two thousand people and reconciled fifteen thousand others under the 'edicts of grace'. His contemporary, Andrés Bernáldez, estimated that in the diocese of Seville alone between 1480 and 1488 the tribunal had burnt over seven hundred people and reconciled more than five thousand, without counting all those who were sentenced to imprisonment. A later historian, the annalist Diego Ortiz de Zúñiga, claimed that in Seville between 1481 and 1524 over twenty thousand heretics had abjured their errors, and over a thousand obstinate heretics had been sent to the stake.

There is little doubt that the figures are exaggerated. The total number of persons passing through the hands of the inquisitors, however, certainly ran into the thousands. The Toledo tribunals may have dealt with over eight thousand cases in the period 1481–1530. The overwhelming majority of these were not in fact brought to trial; they were disciplined as a result of the edicts of grace, and had to undergo various penalties and penances, but escaped with their lives. Trial cases were very much fewer. In them, the penalty of death was pronounced for the most part against specific absent refugees. Effigies, which were burnt in their place, may form part of the total figures for executions given by early chroniclers. The direct penalty of death for heresy was in fact suffered by a very much smaller number than historians had thought. A recent carefully considered view is that in these years of the high tide of persecution, the tribunal of Saragossa had some one hundred and thirty executions in person, that of Valencia possibly some two hundred and twenty-five, that of Barcelona some thirty-four.

In Castile the incidence of executions was probably higher. In the auto de fe at Ciudad Real on 23 February 1484, thirty people were burnt alive and forty in effigy; in the auto at Valladolid on 5 January 1492, thirty-two were burnt alive. The executions were, however, sporadic and concentrated only in the early years. In rounded terms, it is likely that over three-quarters of all those who perished under the Inquisition in the three centuries of its existence, did so in the first half-century. Lack of documentation, however, makes it impossible to arrive at totally reliable figures. One good estimate, based on documentation of the autos de fe, is that 250 people were burnt in person in the Toledo tribunal between 1485 and 1501. Since this tribunal and that of Seville and Jaén were among the few in Castile to have had an intense level of activity, it would not be improbable to suggest a figure five times higher, around one thousand persons, as a rough total for those executed in the tribunals of Castile in the early period. Taking into account all the tribunals of Spain up to about 1530, it is unlikely that more than two thousand people were executed for heresy by the Inquisition.

The final death toll may have been smaller than historians once believed, but the overall impact was certainly devastating for the cultural minorities most directly affected. The reign of terror had an inevitable consequence. Conversos ceased to come forward to admit their errors. Instead, they were forced to take refuge in the very beliefs and practices that they and their parents had turned their backs on. Active Judaism, which existed among some conversos, seems to have been caused primarily by the awakening of their consciousness under persecution. Under pressure, they reverted to the faith of their ancestors. A Jewish lady living in Sigüenza was surprised in 1488 to encounter a man whom she had known previously in Valladolid as a Christian. He now professed to be a Jew, and was begging for charity among the Jews. 'What are you doing over here'? she asked him. 'The Inquisition is around and will burn you'. He answered: 'I want to go to Portugal'. After no doubt equivocating for many years, he had made his decision and was going to risk all for it.

Since conversos occupied a significant place in administration, the professions and trade, diminishing numbers through persecution and emigration must have had a considerable impact on areas of Spain where they had been numerous. . . . The persecution of the conversos was far more damaging to the economy than the later and more spectacular expulsion of the Jews. The latter, because of their marginal status, had played a smaller role in key sectors of public life and controlled fewer economic resources.

Reasons for Inquisition

The wish to eliminate the conversos from public life was, it has been argued, the main reason for the establishment of the Inquisition, and religion was never a genuine motive. In the process, the tribunal and the crown would get rich on the proceeds from confiscations. The argument is plausible, particularly if we deny that there was any widespread judaizing movement among conversos. But, as we shall see, other issues were also involved, making it difficult to accept anti-converso greed as the only motive. Moreover, [King] Ferdinand who always continued to employ conversos in his service, vigorously denied any hostility to them. . . .

The founding of the Inquisition has often been cited as evidence that the Catholic monarchs desired to impose uniformity of religion on Spain. The expulsion of the Jews would seem to confirm it. The monarchs, as fervent Catholics, certainly wished the nation to be united in faith. But there is no evidence at all of a deliberate policy to impose uniformity. Throughout the first decade of the Inquisition's career, Ferdinand and Isabella did not cease to protect their Jews while simultaneously trying to eliminate judaizing among the conversos. Even after the expulsion of the Jews, the Mudéjars [Muslims] remained in full enjoyment of their freedom of religion—in Castile for another decade, in Aragon for another thirty years. The ruthless drive against 'heresy', far from aiming at unification, was no more than the culmination of a long period of social and political pressure directed against the conversos. . . .

If the idea that conversos were secret Jews is to be sustained principally by the evidence dug up by the Inquisition during the 1480s, there can be no doubt of the verdict. Very little convincing proof of Jewish belief or practice among the conversos can be found in the trials. There is no need to question the sincerity of the inquisitors, or to imagine that they maliciously fabricated evidence. It is true that, in the beginning at least, they were not trained lawyers, nor did they have a very clear idea of Jewish religious practice. But they themselves were instruments of a judicial system in which social pressures and prejudices, expressed through unsupported oral testimony, were given virtually unquestioned validity. Those convicted of judaizing fall into three main categories. First, there were those condemned on the evidence of members of the same family. Where this happened, the charges usually appear plausible, though personal quarrels were evidently involved. Second, there were those condemned in their absence. Here the automatic presumption of guilt, the lack of any defence, and the fact that property of the accused was confiscated, tend to make the evidence unacceptable. Third, there were those condemned on the hearsay of often malicious neighbours, most of whom had to reach back in their memory between ten and fifty years in order to find incriminating evidence.

Protestant Reformers Break away from the Catholic Church

Madeleine A. Gray

By the sixteenth century the church had achieved great power and influence in Western Europe. However, some were not happy with the direction the church was taking. In October 1517 Martin Luther, a young Augustinian friar, nailed his "95 Theses," or list of grievances about the church, to the door of a cathedral in the small town of Wittenberg, Germany. His 95 Theses detailed the complaints he had about church practices—in particular, the selling of indulgences. This practice had been established to allow people the absolution of past sins in exchange for monetary contributions. "Sinners" could thereby reduce the time they would have to spend in purgatory recompensing for their sin. Luther opposed the selling of indulgences, arguing that it was by faith alone that people were saved—not by works or actions. His 95 Theses soon became the center of an immense controversy that eventually led to what is now known as the Protestant Reformation. In the following selection, historian Madeleine A. Gray describes the history of the church's practice of indulgences and Luther's opposition to it. She writes that in the view of Luther and other Protestant reformers, it was blasphemous to believe that any action carried out by humans could win favor in God's eyes. In their view, to achieve salvation people had to have faith and trust in God's forgiveness.

Madeleine Gray is a lecturer in history at the University of Wales College, Newport. She is the author of Images of Piety: The Iconography of Traditional Religion in Late Medieval Wales.

Much of the recent historical writing on the Reformation has concentrated on the debate over the alleged shortcomings of the late medieval church, the extent to which it served or failed to serve the needs of the majority of the population, and the extent to which the spiritual lives of ordinary people were affected by the changes of the sixteenth century. For many of the early reformers, this would have been to mistake the incidentals for the central issue. Martin Luther was initially a loyal member of the Catholic church, a monk who taught theology in a fairly traditional university. He had no fundamental quarrel with the personnel or administration of the church. At the outset, his concerns were entirely theological. Even later in his life, when he was more prepared to attack the life and morals of the Catholic church, he insisted that moral reform was useless without reform of doctrine. He had reached the inescapable conclusion that what some representatives of the church were teaching about the way to attain salvation was wrong. In order to understand why, it is necessary to understand how Christians regard sin, and what they mean by salvation. It will also be necessary to look in some detail at the way in which the medieval church dealt with sin and its consequences in order to understand why Luther's ideas met with such opposition.

Ideas of Sin and Salvation in the Medieval Church

For the Christian, sin is not an act: it is a state of being. The medieval church explained it with the Biblical story, of Adam, Eve and the apple. The first humans lived in Paradise, but were forbidden to eat the fruit of the tree of knowledge of good and evil. The Devil tempted Eve, who gave the fruit to her husband Adam. Humans thus became aware of sin, and could not escape its consequence, which was damnation. The resulting fall from grace—the Fall—led to original sin, the state of sin from which individual sins flow.

The Jewish faith, in which Christianity was rooted, had a strong concept of sacrifice and atonement. However, no human sacrifice could really compensate for original sin, since humans were already flawed by original sin. The solution which Christianity offers for this problem is to postulate a human being, Jesus Christ, who is also God. He shares human nature and human temptations but is nevertheless perfect. He can therefore provide a sacrifice which is capable of paying for all human sin. This is what happens in the Biblical account of the Crucifixion. Through Christ's atonement, God and sinful humanity can be reconciled. Although humans are still sinful, they can as a result of Christ's sacrifice be saved. They are made righteous in God's sight and can thus engage in a right relationship with him. It is this process of being made righteous and entering into a right relationship with God which is summed up in the word "justification".

Where the Christian denominations differ (and where Christian doctrine has varied over time) is on the question of how humans can take advantage of that one atoning sacrifice—how they can be justified. The doctrine of the early church, exemplified in the letters of St Paul and the writings of Augustine of Hippo, was that human nature was too damaged by the Fall to be able to work towards salvation. Salvation could come only from God's free gift of grace. The alternative was the idea put forward by Pelagius [an ascetic monk c. 354–c. 420/440], that fallen humanity could still deserve to be saved by its own acts. This was denounced by Augustine as heresy. However, Augustine's doctrine left the individual sinner with no guidance on how to live a Christian life. The consensus in the late medieval church, in practice if not in theory, was that fallible humans should do their best—*quod in se est* was the Latin phrase—and that God in his grace had promised that he would accept their efforts and make up their deficiencies.

There was still room for debate over how far God's initial grace was necessary in order to enable humans to do their best, and how far humans, sinful though they were, could co-operate in the process of salvation. The councils of the early church had failed to provide a theologically watertight definition of justification, the process of reconciliation following Christ's sacrifice. By the late medieval period, opinions were so diverse as to lead writers like Alister McGrath to talk of a crisis of authority on the subject. The majority still adhered to the covenant theory: the view that God had promised to bestow grace on all those who did their best. But an increasing minority—many of them members of the Augustinian religious order which Luther himself joined—considered that humans were too depraved to be able to help themselves. For these theologians, God's grace was necessary *before* the sinner could be justified. . . .

Removal of Consequences of Sin

What the medieval church offered lay people was a framework within which the consequences of original sin were partly removed by the sacrament of baptism, the ritual washing of a young baby (or in unusual cases an adult) with consecrated water. The individual would nevertheless continue to sin. These sins were dealt with by the forgiveness which God channelled through the church. Sins were confessed before a priest who was then empowered to pronounce God's absolution. The sinner was required to be truly penitent; and penitence and the willingness to repent, in theory, required divine grace. However, authors of practical books of guidance on counselling and confession suggested that the sinner who did not experience perfect sorrow or contrition, but who nevertheless went to confession in accordance with God's commands, would then be helped to forgiveness by divine grace.

Absolution was only part of the process. The sinner was also required to make recompense for the sin. This might involve a practical remedy for the consequences of a sin which affected another person—restoring the stolen goods, mending the broken fences, marrying the pregnant girl. But sin was first and foremost an offence against God, so recompense was offered to God by penitential acts. These could range from the repetition of a sequence of prayers to a barefoot pilgrimage to the Holy Land. As it was reasonable to make financial recompense to the earthly victims of sin, so it seemed reasonable that recompense to God might be financial—by paying for candles in a church, for the repair of a church building, for the building of a new church.

Penance not done in the sinner's lifetime would have to be undergone after death, in a place of torment called Purgatory, a sort of little Hell but for a finite period of time. The Church claimed the right to remit time in Purgatory, offering "indulgences" which did not remove the need for confession and contrition but reduced the time which had to be spent in Purgatory making recompense for sin. Again, it seemed reasonable to allow the families of the deceased to buy indulgences on behalf of their dead relatives. Thus it was that, by steps each of which seemed logical and necessary, the medieval church reached the situation in which remission of the penalties of sin was up for sale to the highest bidder. From this it was only a short step to the sale of absolution itself: the distinction between remission of sins and remission of penalties was easy to blur and to misunderstand. . . .

Martin Luther

The future reformer Martin Luther was thus part of a growing trend when, as a young monk, he realized that he could find no assurance of salvation in the rigorous performance of the austerities of the monastic lifestyle. Historians of the Reformation are still divided over the precise path by which he came to his rediscovery of the doctrine of divine grace, or the exact time at which he reached it. Like many an academic, he seems to have reached a new understanding of his subject by explaining it to his students. As professor of biblical studies at the new university of Wittenberg [Germany], he lectured on a series of books of the Bible—the Psalms and the epistles to the Romans, Galatians and Hebrews. It was during the preparation of these lectures that he reached his theological breakthrough. From seeing the righteousness of God as a threat of condemnation and punishment, he came to interpret it as the righteousness which God gives to sinful humans. . . .

This, then, was one of the defining beliefs of the Protestant Reformation: that sinful humanity is totally unable to do anything about its sinfulness, but that God in his infinite mercy has wiped the slate clean. It is what the Protestant means by the crucial concept of justification. To be justified is to be (or to become) virtuous in God's eyes, in order to be able to enter into a right relationship with him. For Luther and those who came after him, it was not only wrong but blasphemous to suggest that any amount of human effort could make anyone virtuous in God's eyes. Only God himself could do that. All that humans had to do—all that humans could do—was to have faith in God's forgiveness. . . .

What was different about Luther's revelation was the use he made of it. While his fellow-Augustinians [the religious order to which Luther belonged] had been prepared to treat the doctrine of justifying grace as a matter for academic debate, Luther saw it in terms of his pastoral responsibility to the parishioners of the Wittenberg churches in his care. For Luther, their reliance on prayers to the saints, pilgrimages and indulgences to save their souls was not only ineffectual, it was actively wrong. They were claiming for themselves a power which belonged only to God. . . .

Zwingli

The Zürich priest Huldrych Zwingli arrived at a similar conclusion about the primacy of faith in salvation but from a rather different starting-point. His first concern was with the multiplicity of observances which were imposed by the church in the name of salvation—prayers, rituals, restrictions on eating, restrictions on sexual activity. Zwingli's initial conclusion was that these observances might be useful but they were not necessary: they had to proceed from personal decision and commitment rather than compulsion. It was the faith which led to these actions which was important. He went on to develop this argument into a more systematic criticism of the rituals which the church imposed on believers. For Zwingli, the only binding observances were those which God asked for in the Bible. Anything else was a human invention, and to depend on human inventions was idolatry. "It is false religion or piety when trust is put in any other than God. They, then, who trust in any created thing whatsoever are not truly pious." True religion "is that which clings to the one and only God" [Zwingli argued]. . . .

Freed by God's gift of righteousness from their terror of sin and its consequences, humans were regenerated, born again into a new life. It was only after this that they were able properly to repent their sins. Contrition was not the means of justification: contrition followed grace and justification. Only then were Christians free to do willingly what they had been unable to do when the moral code of the church commanded it. . . .

The Reformers and Their Ideas on Salvation

There was always a danger that faith would become something which the Christian tried to achieve, and would be regarded as a "good work." Luther and Zwingli both stressed that faith came from God—"the pledge and seal with which God seals our hearts . . . the work of the Spirit in the believer." For [Strasbourg reformer] Bucer, too, God "gives us this conviction and undoubting confidence." "Everything is to be attributed to divine goodness, and nothing to our merit."

But if faith comes from God, and if God's grace is irresistible, why does he not give the gift of faith to everyone? Why are all people not saved?

The answer which some of the Reformers were compelled to give to this question is one of the most difficult doctrines of the Reformation. If faith comes only from God, and if faith is not given to all, then God must have chosen to give faith to some and not to others. Thus, effectively, he has chosen to save some people and to damn others. This [French Christian theologian] doctrine, known as *predestination*, is frequently attributed to Calvin but is inherent in the thinking of some of the earlier reformers. Luther and those who followed him most closely continued to emphasize the freedom of the human will and to argue that the doctrine of predestination effectively made God responsible for evil and human sin. However, as early as 1523, the Strasbourg reformer Martin Bucer was prepared to divide all humanity into the *elect*, those who God had already chosen for salvation, and the damned or *reprobate*. He later made clear that this separation took place before birth. It could have nothing to do with human actions or human goodness. Salvation was entirely dependent on God's free choice, made before the foundation of the world.

The Catholic Counterreformation

John C. Dwyer

John C. Dwyer holds a doctorate in theology from the University of Tubingen, Germany. He served for many years as a professor of theology at St. Mary's College in Moraga, California, and is presently teaching theology and scripture at St. Bernard's Institute, Graduate School of Theology and Ministry, in Albany, New York. In the following excerpt from his book Church History: Twenty Centuries of Catholic Christianity, *Dwyer examines the Catholic Reformation movement of the sixteenth century, which was dedicated to improving the administration and discipline of the church. He argues that the Catholic Reformation was a direct reaction to the Protestant Reformation that began in 1517 when Augustinian monk Martin Luther publicly opposed the Church's practice of selling "indulgences" or the promise of absolution of people's sins in exchange for money. The Protestants emphasized that salvation could only come through faith, not through good works or actions—or through the authority of the Catholic Church. The Catholic Reformation was a period of internal renewal and revival.*

Dwyer also describes the creation during this period of the religious order of the Society of Jesus, commonly known as Jesuits. Bound by their complete obedience to the pope and marked by their intellectual rigor and energy, the Jesuits were at the forefront of the Catholic resistance to Protestant reform. According to Dwyer, the Jesuits effectively pushed back the tide of Protestantism by establishing Jesuit colleges and spreading the Gospel. Dwyer also asserts that the Catholic Reformation gave rise to a new concept of spirituality that emphasized the humanity of Christ.

Jesuits and other new Christian religious orders began to devote themselves to acts of charity for the poor and the uneducated in cities and towns.

Historians often argue about whether this period should be called the *Counterreformation* or the *Catholic Reform*. Each of these terms points to something important about the period, and yet each is also incomplete. The word *Counterreformation* often has a pejorative sense and implies that the papacy attempted, with the aid of the absolutist Catholic monarchies of southern Europe and with the help of the Jesuits, to recover the terrain lost to the [Protestant] Reformation and to restore the discredited institutions of the pre-Reformation period. But if the term is stripped of these somewhat naive connotations, it can be a useful description of the period. For it is true that although the Catholic renewal of the sixteenth century had begun very tentatively before 1517, it developed in opposition to the Reformation, and at the Council of Trent [1545–63] the Catholic church defined itself by the emphatic rejection of the major, theses of Reformation theology.

Achievements of the Catholic Counterreformation

Catholic Reform is a useful term, but it seems to imply that the reform of the one church in head and members, which [Protestant reformer Martin] Luther and the other reformers desired but failed to bring about, was achieved within the Catholic church itself in the course of the sixteenth and seventeenth centuries. But what happened during these centuries was not restricted to reform, as that word had been understood about the year 1500; and the church which emerged from the Council of Trent or, more accurately, the church which was a product of the Tridentine reform, was not simply purified of certain abuses. Rather, it was a much more tightly organized, and distinctively Latin church, which defined itself not only against the Reformation, but also against the concerns and the character of northern European Christianity. And yet, particularly during the sixteenth and the early part of the seventeenth century, the church did rid itself of many of the abuses against which the reformers had protested. And when the reform movement reached the papacy shortly before the middle of the sixteenth century, the church was given an entirely new shape and form as a result of the work of these reforming Popes.

Probably the best way to describe what happened to the Catholic church during this period would be to speak of retrenchment and renewal: a defensive step backward to regroup, reorganize, and tighten the chain of command, in order to confront an enemy who had appeared unexpectedly, and in order to win back ground lost in the initial moment of the surprise attack. For initially, the Catholic church reacted to the outbreak of the Reformation with something very much like paralysis: the Popes were indecisive and fearful; the emperor vacillated between, on the one hand, wanting Luther burned at the stake, and, on the other, asking that Rome agree to almost all of the Lutheran demands; religious houses emptied almost overnight; and half of Christendom seceded without any real opposition.

Jesuits at the Forefront of Catholic Reform

Religious life (in the sense of giving up marriage and the right to dispose of personal property, and doing this "for the sake of the kingdom") has always developed its concrete forms in response to the needs of the church at a particular moment of history, and in response to the signs of the times. And so it was at the time of the Reformation. The papacy was under attack, and Catholics seemed paralyzed by the intellectual and moral vigor of the reformers; but at this very moment a religious order was founded which made absolute obedience to the Pope its distinguishing mark, and which from the beginning exhibited an enormous intellectual energy which catapulted its members into the leadership both of the Counterreformation and of the Catholic Reform. In fact, the success story of the Jesuits during this period is virtually the key to understanding the history of the church from about 1540 to 1700.

Ignatius was born in 1491 in a family of the Basque nobility. . . .

While studying theology at the University, Ignatius continued to cultivate the life of prayer and asceticism, and he continued to work on his little book of *Spiritual Exercises*. Others began to gather around him and under his direction they made the *Spiritual Exercises* and dedicated their lives to God— the goal which the Exercises sought. On August 15, 1534, Ignatius and six dedicated followers took private vows of poverty and chastity and joined to these a promise to go to the Holy Land and work there for the conversion of the Moslems. Prudently, Ignatius specified that if the Holy Land venture should prove impossible, the members of his little group would put themselves at the disposition of the Pope and commit themselves to whatever task he gave them.

When one obstacle after another appeared in the way of their journey to the Holy Land, they took this as a sign from God, and in 1539 Ignatius formally requested the Pope, Paul III, to grant his approval for a new religious order. This order would be distinguished by the absence of most of the practices which were part of the life of the older religious orders: common recitation of the Office (the public prayer of the church), living in cloister, distinctive garb, prescribed mortifications, and many others. This new order would be mobile, able to go at a moment's notice to the ends of the earth in the fulfillment of that vow which was its really distinguishing mark—absolute obedience to the Pope in undertaking whatever apostolate he assigned them. In 1539 Paul III approved the new order and in 1540 the official document of approval was issued. The Jesuit order was formally in existence. . . .

Jesuits Push Back Against Protestantism

Ignatius had not founded his order to combat the Reformation, but the intellectual training of his men and their dedication to the papacy made it inevitable that they would be in the forefront of the Catholic resistance to the Reformation. When the Council of Trent finally did meet, Jesuit theologians played a leading role, and they insisted that no concessions be made to the Protestants, thus giving the Council its distinctive character. At a time when much of Europe was turning from the papacy, the Jesuits bound themselves by a special vow of obedience to the Pope, and they were instrumental in creating the *papal* church of the modern world. In those areas where the Counterreformation was successful, this was achieved to a significant degree through the founding of Jesuit colleges, because these institutions were established, not only in the Catholic heartland, but also in those areas which had been partially lost to the Reformation. The German, Peter Canisius, joined the order in 1543, and successfully led the campaign to keep southern Germany loyal to the Catholic church. He wrote a catechism for Catholics which was in use up to the present century.

Later in the century, Robert Bellarmine, the Italian Jesuit (1542 to 1621), became the first to make the church itself an object of theological study. A skilled controversialist, he undertook to prove that the reformers were wrong in their understanding of the church. In this attempt he strongly emphasized the social and juridical dimension of the church, and defined it in a way which underlined the points which distinguished Catholics from Protestants. In this, Bellarmine was simply continuing a tradition which had been begun by Jesuit theologians at Trent, who urged that the Council make a statement of Catholic doctrine which would be devoid of any spirit of compromise with the teaching of the reformers, and which would define Catholic doctrine in decidedly anti-Protestant terms. . . .

Jesuits first became involved with schools about two decades after the order was founded. The practical needs of the time fostered a growing involvement in this apostolate, and the Jesuit colleges in Germany were a major weapon in winning back territory from the Protestants and in stopping the advance of the Reformation in southern Germany. In 1585 an important document was published, which has guided Jesuit education almost to the present day: the *Ratio Studiorum* or Plan of Studies. It is a clear statement of dedication to the principles of humanistic education, and on the basis of this document the Jesuits became the teachers of the European elite, not only in Catholic countries but in some lands which had gone over to the Reformation and in others which were nominally under the control of the Russian Orthodox Church.

But Jesuits were not simply pragmatic educators; the order fielded a number of creative artists as well. Jesuit architecture and theater were an expression of the Baroque spirit, which is itself a key to understanding the dynamism and appeal of the Catholic reawakening. Finally, as Europe turned its face outward again, to the newly discovered lands of the Far East, it was Jesuit missionaries who scored the greatest successes, and who approached the ancient cultures of that part of the world with an openness and sympathy which might have led to the conversion of entire populations if it had not been for the jealousy of some of the other orders and the tragic stupidity of some of the Popes of the eighteenth century.

A New Concept of Spirituality Comes into Being

More than in most other periods, the life of the church during this time of reawakening can be described by a word which usually refers to an architectural or musical style. But the Baroque period was more than a time when a certain artistic style was dominant; rather it was a time which brought a new way of looking at the human situation, a new appreciation of the hierarchical order of the world, and a new attempt to unify all creation in such a view. This Baroque worldview found expression in almost every area of life. . . .

In a sense, none of this was really new. The High Middle Ages had certainly had a hierarchical view of the world, and the Popes of the thirteenth century were absolute both in their pretensions to power and in their exercise of it. But for the Baroque period, there was a difference. God and his world of heavenly beings (angels and saints) were no longer on the other side of a great divide. Rather, a *channel* had been opened between heaven and earth and a vision of heaven became possible for human beings below. The light from this vision streamed into the churches of the Baroque era and flooded the devotional life of Catholics of that period. In the Baroque church (in both senses: the building and the institution), the men and women of Catholic Europe left the drabness of the world behind, and they were offered an emotional and even ecstatic encounter with God. The Gesù, the Jesuit mother church in Rome, and all of the other churches which were built in imitation of it, are the artistic expression of this vision.

But when a vision of heaven becomes possible from within this world, there is an element injected into human life which cannot be grasped by merely rational analysis. There is something about the fascinating but awe-inspiring reality of God which must be *felt* and which makes a strong appeal to *emotion*. Ignatius' *Spiritual Exercises* demonstrates this: it was the Jesuit order which brought intellectual vigor to the Counterreformation, but an important part of the meditative prayer of the Jesuit is the "application of the senses" in which the one who prays uses all of the resources of senses and imagination to understand the call of Christ and to motivate himself to respond: more whole-heartedly.

Because it was Jesus who opened this channel from heaven to earth, the Baroque showed a new interest in the humanity of Jesus. The Sacred Heart devotion became popular after the visions which were experienced by a French nun, Margaret Mary Alacoque, between 1673 and 1675: this devotion is typically Baroque in its emphasis on the humanity and vulnerability of Jesus and on the strong appeal to the senses which characterizes the art (and pseudo-art) associated with it.

Baroque Christianity was interested in preaching the Gospel to ordinary people, to the very groups which had been neglected in earlier periods. This did not spring from any hidden democratic tendencies of the Baroque world—its vision was far too hierarchical for that—but it did come from the increased attention being given to the humanity of Christ, and it expressed itself in the preaching and charitable work of Vincent de Paul (+ 1660) and in the dedication to educating young men of the poorer classes which found expression in the founding of the Christian Brothers by John Baptist de la Salle, who lived from 1651 to 1719.

During the period of the Baroque, religion became a joyous and even exuberant exercise. There was nothing somber about a Baroque church: beauty was consciously sought, not for its own sake, but because it manifested the glory of God. The practice of religion was made attractive to the senses in every way, and it offered relief from the drabness of life. In the Jesuit colleges great attention was given to drama and Jesuit playwrights produced their own dramas in order to drive home the central points of the theology of the Catholic Reform. . . .

Reforms Prior to the Council of Trent

In 1540 Paul III had given his approval to the Jesuits, and other orders were founded in the same century. After the Jesuits, it was the Capuchins who had the greatest impact. They spread rapidly, and by about 1650 there were twenty thousand Capuchins living throughout western Europe, from Ireland to Poland, with their greatest strength in the Latin countries, and especially in Italy. They took as their goal the full observance of the Franciscan rule, and they undertook to live in poverty and to bring the Gospel to the people in the cities and villages of Italy. They probably were a major factor in the failure of the Reformation to make much headway there, and they have been popular as confessors and preachers of missions up to the present day.

The Enlightenment's Challenge to Catholicism

Jonathan Hill

Although science had its genesis in the scholastic endeavors of Catholic monks in medieval universities, in the eighteenth century reason was to replace faith as the sole arbiter of truth and knowledge. This era was known as the Enlightenment, or the Age of Rationalism. To these enlightened thinkers, faith was a myth that had long outlived its place in rational discourse. No longer was man dependent on revelation to make known the mysteries of the universe. In the following excerpt from his work Faith in the Age of Reason: The Enlightenment from Galileo to Kant, *Jonathan Hill explores and analyzes the differing views and ideas held by rationalists in the eighteenth century and the effect of this new philosophy on Catholic teachings. Hill argues that philosophers and intellectuals in the eighteenth century believed that all knowledge, including the fundamental truths of Christianity, was accessible to all men through the power of reason. This claim, he argues, became problematic for the Catholic church. Beginning in the Middle Ages, the church taught that while reason and faith could coexist, it was only through revelation that man could come to know and recognize eternal truths.*

Hill writes that medieval intellectuals believed that although there were different categories of knowledge, each with its own means of "enquiry," these branches of knowledge constituted one unified whole. The philosophers of the Enlightenment, he argues, sought to disrupt and dismantle this unified system of thought, which in turn gave rise to new and differing ideas and modes of thinking and understanding, such as those of René Descartes,

Jonathan Hill, "Faith, Reason and Authority," in *Faith in the Age of Reason: The Enlightenment from Galileo to Kant*. Downers, IL: Intervarsity Press, 2004, pp. 113–35. Copyright © 2004 Jonathan Hill. This edition copyright © Lion Hudson. All rights reserved. In the U.S. reproduced by permission of Intervarsity Press. In the U.K. reproduced by permission of Lion Hudson, PLC.

John Locke, Michel de Montaigne, and other eighteenth-century philosophers and intellectuals.

Jonathan Hill graduated with a BA in philosophy and theology and an MA in theology from Oriel College, Oxford, in 1997, where he specialized in Leibniz and the Church Fathers. Hill is the author of The History of Christian Thought *and* What Has Christianity Ever Done for Us?

The one thing that rationalists and empiricists had in common was that they both believed that knowledge was accessible through the use of human faculties. In the second chapter of his *Discourse on Method*, [French philosopher René] Descartes presented four rules that he had deduced to ensure correct reasoning. He tells us the first of these:

> I would not accept anything as true which I did not clearly know to be true. That is to say, I would carefully avoid being over hasty or prejudiced, and I would understand nothing by my judgments beyond what presented itself so clearly and distinctly to my mind that I had no occasion to doubt it.

Reason Is the Source of Truth and Knowledge

Here we have the essence of rationalism, the notion that the truth of an idea can be ascertained by considering the nature of that idea. But Descartes' principle is all-encompassing: he will accept as true *nothing*, that he cannot *know* to be true in this way. Done thoroughly, this results in the method of doubt . . . and among the things that are doubted and then assessed by reason in this way are religious claims. In other words, in Descartes' world, reason is the final arbiter of what is true. We cannot take anything to be true simply on authority, whether that is the authority of the Bible, of the church or of tradition.

As we might expect, this notion is part and parcel of philosophical rationalism. If you can construct a system of metaphysics, and ethics on the basis of a few self-evident postulates, as [Dutch philosopher Benedict de] Spinoza attempted to do, then there is little place for traditional authority—and indeed, one of the things Spinoza got into trouble for was his pioneering work in biblical criticism, the attempt to understand the Bible as a product of human history rather than as a divine revelation. And what could be more inimical to the traditional authorities than [German mathematician Gottfried Wilhem] Leibniz's hope that, one day, all disagreements would be resolved with little more than 'Let us calculate'?

Revelation Subject to Rational Scrutiny

This approach was rapidly becoming dominant within intellectual circles. It was shared not only by rationalists in the philosophical sense but by empiricists too. In his *Essay Concerning Human Understanding*, [British philosopher] Locke considers the authority at revelation as a potential source of knowledge:

> Whatever God hath revealed, is certainly true; no doubt can be made of it. This is the proper object of faith. But whether it be a divine revelation, or no, reason must judge: which can never permit the mind to reject a greater evidence to embrace what is less evident, nor allow it to entertain probability in opposition to knowledge and certainty (Book IV, chapter 18).

In other words, we can rest assured that divine revelation is true and trustworthy. But we cannot necessarily assume that what we are hearing really *is* divine revelation—and to determine that, it is necessary to look at the evidence and decide for ourselves. So while Locke pays lip service to the importance of revelation, in reality revelation, like any other source of information, must be subject to rational scrutiny.

For Locke himself, this approach was quite compatible with orthodox Christianity, and he spent considerable time not only poring over the scriptures but publishing his thoughts on them, principally in a series of paraphrases of and notes on books of the New Testament, which found a wide readership when published shortly after his death. Indeed, Locke's view of revelation represented an important element of the typically Anglican 'common sense' approach to faith. It was an approach that rejected the authoritarianism that was regarded as one of the chief flaws of Roman Catholicism, and which felt that the reliability of the scriptures, and the truth of orthodox doctrine, would inevitably commend themselves to the individual enquirer through their own merits.

But thinkers such as Locke were starting to push the point in a way that some felt was going, perhaps, a little too far. Locke did it himself in *The Reasonableness of Christianity as Delivered in the Scriptures*, published anonymously in 1695. In this work, to be sure, Locke concluded that the doctrines of orthodox Christianity were true, or at least most of them, and that the Bible is to be trusted. But what angered many was the fact that he felt himself qualified to issue such a judgment in the first place. Wasn't he essentially setting up human reason as the final arbiter of revelation? And didn't this open up the possibility that reason might reject that revelation?

Medieval System of Thought

What was happening during the Enlightenment was essentially the disruption of a unified, organic system of thought that had developed during the Middle Ages. One of the founding principles of that system of thought was the essential agreement between faith and reason—a principle tempered by the equally important one that faith and reason are not equal partners. What reason tells us is correct, but faith tells us more.

This notion of faith 'perfecting' reason is exemplified in the work of Thomas Aquinas, the greatest of the medieval scholastic philosophers. For instance, in his magisterial *Summa*

Theologiae, Aquinas argues that God's existence is certain: indeed, there are five different ways of proving it, through the exercise of reason alone. At the same time, scripture and the revelation that has been given to the church confirms that there is indeed a God. But the information conveyed by revelation is more extensive: it tells us that God is a Trinity, that he became incarnate in Christ, and that he saves us.

Aquinas's influence over Catholicism only increased with the Reformation, as Catholic theologians went back to his work for new inspiration against the Protestants. Funnily enough, despite his status as the pre-eminent medieval Catholic authority; Aquinas was also popular with many Protestants. Theodore Beza, the most significant Reformed theologian after [French reformer John] Calvin himself, was a particular fan. Thus, the approach to faith and reason that Aquinas represented was, by the time of the Enlightenment, deeply entrenched throughout Christendom, both Catholic and Protestant.

Together with this insistence on faith perfecting reason, the medieval thinkers and their successors developed the idea that, although all the different branches of knowledge form a coherent whole, it can still be divided into different disciplines, each of which has its own method of enquiry. For example, it would be inappropriate to use the methods of mathematicians to find out truths of morality; and it would be wrong to expect any moral findings to have the same level of certainty and accuracy as maths. This was a common-sense view that went back to Aristotle.

Enlightenment Ideas Disrupt Medieval System of Thought

The new philosophy was breaking this understanding of human knowledge apart. Descartes' avowed aim to transfer the methods of mathematics to metaphysics and physical science was an assault on the traditional division of the sciences, intensified by Spinoza's choice to present his ethics in a form such as that of a geometry textbook. Yet even more radical than this new approach—which was shocking enough to old-fashioned philosophy professors—was the abandoning of the old understanding of faith and reason that it entailed. If Descartes and Spinoza could really deduce the most subtle doctrines of divine and human nature through the power of mathematics alone, then clearly there was not much need for revelation.

As the new philosophy confronted the old, and gave way in its turn to a variety of new and often radically opposed methodologies, the issue of faith and reason was up for grabs, and a bewildering variety of possibilities became available.

One option was, as far as possible, to hang on to the old way of seeing things. Many found this surprisingly easy throughout the period, and it is a useful reminder of the fact that the Enlightenment was not a matter of a new way of thinking simply replacing the old, but of new ways of thinking jostling for space with the old. . . .

Reason Used to Defend Religion

But reason could play a more proactive role in the defence of religion, and it was now, as the old verities began to crumble, that many felt a new and pressing need for it to do so. Apologetics—the task of presenting Christianity to those outside it—flourished, although it was generally intended to bolster the faithful rather than convert the heathen. A host of pious writers produced books confirming the belief, shared by most people since ancient times, that God's existence and goodness could be proven deductively from an examination of the natural world.

The most thorough and rigorous apologetics of the Enlightenment was that of William Paley. . . .

Paley was convinced that reason could provide a solid support for Christianity. But by this he does not mean the logical deductions of Descartes: he means the rigorous application of the scientific method as exemplified by Newton. Philosophy, for Paley as for the mainstream British tradition since Locke, is a matter of advancing arguments and hypotheses on the basis of what we experience. It is an approach that proceeds on the basis of induction—the notion that there is a basic regularity to the world, and that by observing it we can form general notions that, while not mathematically certain, can have varying degrees of probability.

Paley put this principle into devastating effect with his masterly *Natural Theology*, published to great acclaim in 1802, shortly before his death. It is considered the most powerful statement ever made of what is known as the 'teleological argument' for the existence of God. 'Teleology' means purpose, and Paley argues that a dispassionate examination of the world shows that many natural objects appear designed for a purpose—and this in turn suggests a designer. The argument had been made countless times before, but Paley's originality lay partly in the fact that he provided a cogent defence of its underlying assumption—the supposition that an apparently designed object must have been created by an intelligent designer. . . .

The ideal of men like William Paley was not to replace faith with reason. On the contrary, it was to bolster and reinforce faith. If Locke claimed that reason must decide whether or not a divine revelation has really happened, Paley devoted considerable energy to showing that it had. He believed that his scientific approach to Christianity led not to arid rationalism but to a living, deeply spiritual awareness of God. . .

The Jansenists: Two Distinct Bodies of Knowledge

The staunch traditionalism of thinkers such as Paley was not the only solution available to the problem of how to relate faith to reason.

One alternative was associated with the Jansenists, the Catholic group who believed in predestination. . . .

This position was developed by Antoine Arnauld, the most prominent Jansenist theologian. He was, on the whole, quite an enthusiastic Cartesian, as well as a supporter of modern scientists such as Copernicus and Galileo, and he believed that in matters of philosophy and science reason should be the sole authority. But he did not think that this applied to the theological sphere, and indeed drew a clear distinction between them. When he was writing to Descartes in the 1640s, he would consciously deal with some issues 'as' a philosopher, and with others 'as' a theologian. There are some matters that reason is simply not competent to deal with, and these are things that must be accepted on the authority of the church. That's not to say that reason is simply irrelevant to religious matters—on the contrary, Arnauld thought that many religious disputes are actually about the sphere of nature rather than the sphere of faith, and should be settled by reason, not external authority.

So instead of the medieval belief in a single body of knowledge that could be accessed in two ways—faith and reason—Arnauld suggested two distinct realms of knowledge. This position was dangerous, because it meant that there was a sphere of knowledge that traditional authority had no business addressing. . . .

To those of a more conservative religious nature, such as [Pope] Alexander VII, Arnauld's approach was setting up reason as a rival to revelation and the traditional authority which embodied it. It was becoming clear that a dividing line was being drawn between the two approaches—the reliance on revelation and the reliance on reason—and Arnauld's attempt to defend the authority of reason in some spheres while acknowledging revelation in others would almost inevitably give way to a more radical sort of approach, that anticipated by Descartes, where *everything* falls within the sphere of reason alone. . . .

The Uncertainty of Doubt

Scepticism means simply the opposite of certainty: it is the adoption of a doubting attitude, such as that exemplified by Descartes in his *Meditations*. It had been around for an extremely long time, and had been a powerful element of Greek philosophy. Socrates, the greatest hero of ancient philosophy, had famously claimed to know only that he knew nothing, and other philosophers tried to take this position to extreme lengths, to the extent of declaring not even to know that much.

The godfather of Enlightenment scepticism was Michel de Montaigne, a French aristocrat who lived during the sixteenth century and whose *Essays* were a series of loosely linked meditations upon human nature. Montaigne concluded that human beings were feeble creatures, whose boasts to knowledge and power ultimately came to nothing. His ideas were expanded on by his cousin, Francisco Sanches, a Portuguese philosopher whose *That Nothing Is Known* was published in 1581, and who argued that, in the face of uncertainty about all matters, we must use careful scientific methods to make the most of what we can know.

Ideas like this became extremely popular in the early seventeenth century, and were used to attack the new science and philosophy just as much as they were used to demolish the old scholastic philosophy. . . .

But where Descartes hoped to turn the 'method of doubt' into a tool for discovering metaphysical certainty, others saw in it a powerful weapon of social and ideological criticism. The way was led by Pierre Bayle, whose *Historical and Critical Dictionary* of 1696 was a masterpiece of enlightened scepticism. In his brilliant and entertaining footnotes, Bayle undermined virtually every doctrine he was supposedly describing, by showing how they all led to paradoxes and irrationality. Every theory and claim to certainty, for Bayle, turns out to be arrant nonsense—none more so than the traditional claims of religion. . . .

Little wonder, then, that Bayle's *Dictionary* became so popular among his successors such as Voltaire and the *philosophes*, and that others condemned his ideas as inimical to religion. It was with enlightened scepticism, above all else, that Voltaire would 'crush infamy' in the form of oppressive, superstitious religion. Yet scepticism was such a powerful tool that it would eventually prove too potent even for the *philosophes*.

The Immaculate Conception

Pius IX

Many believe that the term "Immaculate Conception" refers to the conception of Jesus within the womb of Mary. However, the Immaculate Conception in fact refers to Mary's conception within the womb of her mother, St. Anne. In defining the dogma of the Immaculate Conception on December 8, 1854, in the apostolic constitution "Ineffabilis Deus," excerpted below, Pope Pius IX officially proclaims that Mary was preserved by divine grace from the stain of original sin from the moment of her conception. Therefore, unlike the rest of mankind, Mary lived a life completely free from sin. The pope writes that by virtue of her role as the mother of the son of God, it is only fitting that God preserved Mary from original sin so that his son Jesus could be wholly uncontaminated and pure.

Pius IX also argues that the dogma of the Immaculate Conception is not only supported by the writings of preeminent theologians and church fathers, it is also confirmed by holy scripture. In the first chapter of Luke's Gospel, the pope writes, the angel Gabriel's salutation, "Hail Mary, full of Grace," affirms the singular grace that God freely bestowed on Mary so that she could transmit to her divine son the same perfect, undefiled, and worthy human nature. The dogma of the Immaculate Conception remains one of the central tenets of the Catholic faith. The feast of the Immaculate Conception, celebrated by the church on December 8, constitutes a holy day of obligation for Catholics.

God ineffable—whose ways are mercy and truth, whose will is omnipotence itself, and whose wisdom "reaches from end to end mightily, and orders all things sweetly"—having foreseen from all eternity the lamentable wretchedness

Pius IX, "Ineffabilis Deus," apostolic constitution defining the dogma of the Immaculate Conception, Papal Encyclicals Online, December 8, 1854. www.papalencyclicals.net/Pius09/p9ineff.htm.

of the entire human race which would result from the sin of Adam, decreed, by a plan hidden from the centuries, to complete the first work of his goodness by a mystery yet more wondrously sublime through the Incarnation of the Word. This he decreed in order that man who, contrary to the plan of Divine Mercy had been led into sin by the cunning malice of Satan, should not perish; and in order that what had been lost in the first Adam would be gloriously restored in the Second Adam. From the very beginning, and before time began, the eternal Father chose and prepared for his only-begotten Son a Mother in whom the Son of God would become incarnate and from whom, in the blessed fullness of time, he would be born into this world. Above all creatures did God so love her that truly in her was the Father well pleased with singular delight. Therefore, far above all the angels and all the saints so wondrously did God endow her with the abundance of all heavenly gifts poured from the treasury of his divinity that this mother, ever absolutely free of all stain of sin, all fair and perfect, would possess that fullness of holy innocence and sanctity than which, under God, one cannot even imagine anything greater, and which, outside of God, no mind can succeed in comprehending fully.

Grace Bestowed on Mary for Divine Purposes

And indeed it was wholly fitting that so wonderful a mother should be ever resplendent with the glory of most sublime holiness and so completely free from all taint of original sin that she would triumph utterly over the ancient serpent. To her did the Father will to give his only-begotten Son—the Son whom, equal to the Father and begotten by him, the Father loves from his heart—and to give this Son in such a way that he would be the one and the same common Son of God the Father and of the Blessed Virgin Mary. It was she whom the Son himself chose to make his Mother and it was from her that the Holy Spirit willed and brought it about that he should be conceived and born from whom he himself proceeds.

The Catholic Church, directed by the Holy Spirit of God, is the pillar and base of truth and has ever held as divinely revealed and as contained in the deposit of heavenly revelation this doctrine concerning the original innocence of the august Virgin—a doctrine which is so perfectly in harmony with her wonderful sanctity and preeminent dignity as Mother of God—and thus has never ceased to explain, to teach and to foster this doctrine age after age in many ways and by solemn acts. From this very doctrine, flourishing and wondrously propagated in the Catholic world through the efforts and zeal of the bishops, was made very clear by the Church when she did not hesitate to present for the public devotion and veneration of the faithful the Feast of the Conception of the Blessed Virgin. By this most significant fact, the Church made it clear indeed that the conception of Mary is to be venerated as something extraordinary, wonderful, eminently holy, and different from the conception of all other human beings—for the Church celebrates only the feast days of the saints.

And hence the very words with which the Sacred Scriptures speak of Uncreated Wisdom and set forth his eternal origin, the Church, both in its ecclesiastical offices and in its liturgy, has been wont to apply likewise to the origin of the Blessed Virgin, inasmuch as God, by one and the same decree, had established the origin of Mary and the Incarnation of Divine Wisdom. . . .

Immaculate Conception Affirmed by Church Fathers and Holy Scripture

All are aware with how much diligence this doctrine of the Immaculate Conception of the Mother of God has been handed down, proposed and defended by the most outstanding religious orders, by the more celebrated theological academies, and by very eminent doctors in the sciences of theology. All know, likewise, how eager the bishops have been to profess openly and publicly, even in ecclesiastical assemblies, that Mary, the most holy Mother of God, by virtue of the foreseen merits of Christ, our Lord and Redeemer, was never subject to original sin, but was completely preserved from the original taint, and hence she was redeemed in a manner more sublime.

Besides, we must note a fact of the greatest importance indeed. Even the Council of Trent (ecumenical Council, 1545–63) itself, when it promulgated the dogmatic decree concerning original sin, following the testimonies of the Sacred Scriptures, of the Holy Fathers and of the renowned Council, decreed and defined that all men are born infected by original sin; nevertheless, it solemnly declared that it had no intention of including the blessed and immaculate Virgin Mary, the Mother of God, in this decree and in the general extension of its definition. Indeed, considering the times and circumstances, the Fathers of Trent sufficiently intimated by this declaration that the Blessed Virgin Mary was free from the original stain; and thus they clearly signified that nothing could be reasonably cited from the Sacred Scriptures, from Tradition, or from the authority of the Fathers, which would in any way be opposed to so great a prerogative of the Blessed Virgin. . . .

Interpreters of the Sacred Scripture

The Fathers and writers of the Church, well versed in the heavenly Scriptures, had nothing more at heart than to vie with one another in preaching and teaching in many wonderful ways the Virgin's supreme sanctity, dignity, and immunity from all stain of sin, and her renowned victory over the most foul enemy of the human race. This they did in the books they wrote to explain the Scriptures, to vindicate the dogmas, and to instruct the faithful. These ecclesiastical writers in quoting the words by which at the beginning of the world God announced his merciful remedies prepared for the regeneration of mankind—words by which he crushed the audacity of the deceitful serpent and wondrously raised up the hope of our race, saying, "I will put enmities between you and the woman, between your seed and her seed" [Gn 3:15]—taught that by this divine prophecy the merciful Redeemer of mankind, Jesus Christ, the only begotten Son of God, was clearly foretold: That his most Blessed Mother, the Virgin Mary, was prophetically indicated; and, at the same time, the very enmity of both against the evil one was significantly expressed. Hence, just as Christ, the Mediator between God and man, assumed human nature, blotted the handwriting of the decree that stood against us, and fastened it triumphantly to the cross, so the most holy Virgin, united with him by a most intimate and indissoluble bond, was, with him and through him, eternally at enmity with the evil serpent, and most completely triumphed over him, and thus crushed his head with her immaculate foot. . . .

The Annunciation

When the Fathers and writers of the Church meditated on the fact that the most Blessed Virgin was, in the name and by order of God himself, proclaimed full of grace by the Angel Gabriel when he announced her most sublime dignity of Mother of God, they thought that this singular and solemn salutation, never heard before, showed that the Mother of God is the seat of all divine graces and is adorned with all gifts of the Holy Spirit. To them Mary is an almost infinite treasury, an inexhaustible abyss of these gifts, to such an extent that she was never subject to the curse and was, together with her Son, the only partaker of perpetual benediction. Hence she was worthy to hear Elizabeth, inspired by the Holy Spirit, exclaim: "Blessed are you among women, and blessed is the fruit of your womb" [Cf. Lk 1:28].

Hence, it is the clear and unanimous opinion of the Fathers that the most glorious Virgin, for whom "he who is mighty has done great things," was resplendent with such an abundance of heavenly gifts, with such a fullness of grace and with such innocence, that she is an unspeakable miracle of God—indeed, the crown of all miracles and truly the Mother of God; that she approaches as near to God himself as is possible for a created being; and that she is above all men and angels in glory. Hence, to demonstrate the original innocence and sanctity of the Mother of God, not only did they frequently compare her to Eve while yet a virgin, while yet innocence, while yet incorrupt, while not yet deceived by the deadly snares of the most treacherous serpent; but they have also exalted her above Eve with a wonderful variety of expressions. Eve listened to the serpent with lamentable consequences; she fell from original innocence and became his slave. The most Blessed Virgin, on the contrary, ever increased her original gift, and not only never lent an ear to the serpent, but by divinely given power she utterly destroyed the force and dominion of the evil one. . . .

The Pronouncement

Wherefore, in humility and fasting, we unceasingly offered our private prayers as well as the public prayers of the Church to God the Father through his Son, that he would deign to direct and strengthen our mind by the power of the Holy Spirit. In like manner did we implore the help of the entire heavenly host as we ardently invoked the Paraclete [Holy Spirit]. Accordingly, by the inspiration of the Holy Spirit, for the honor of the Holy and undivided Trinity, for the glory and adornment of the Virgin Mother of God, for the exaltation of the Catholic Faith, and for the furtherance of the Catholic religion, by the authority of Jesus Christ our Lord, of the Blessed Apostles Peter and Paul, and by our own: "We declare, pronounce, and define that the doctrine which holds that the most Blessed Virgin Mary, in the first instance of her conception, by a singular grace and privilege granted by Almighty

God, in view of the merits of Jesus Christ, the Savior of the human race, was preserved free from all stain of original sin, is a doctrine revealed by God and therefore to be believed firmly and constantly by all the faithful." . . .

Let all the children of the Catholic Church, who are so very dear to us, hear these words of ours. With a still more ardent zeal for piety, religion and love, let them continue to venerate, invoke and pray to the most Blessed Virgin Mary, Mother of God, conceived without original sin. Let them fly with utter confidence to this most sweet Mother of mercy and grace in all dangers, difficulties, needs, doubts and fears. Under her guidance, under her patronage, under her kindness and protection, nothing is to be feared; nothing is hopeless. Because, while bearing toward us a truly motherly affection and having in her care the work of our salvation, she is solicitous about the whole human race. And since she has been appointed by God to be the Queen of heaven and earth, and is exalted above all the choirs of angels and saints, and even stands at the right hand of her only-begotten Son, Jesus Christ our Lord, she presents our petitions in a most efficacious manner. What she asks, she obtains. Her pleas can never be unheard.

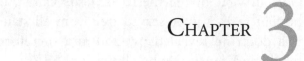

CHAPTER 3

The Catholic Church in the Twentieth Century

The Debate over the Church's Role During World War II

John Davis and Robert McCormick

Known for his political skills, the election of Pope Pius XII on March 2, 1939, left many confident that in an era of great uncertainty, he was indeed the man to lead the church. Pius XII, however, has become one of the most controversial figures in history. At issue is whether the pope, as the moral authority of the Catholic church, did enough to protect the Jews from the Nazi genocide during World War II. In the following article, "The Role of Pope Pius XII in the Holocaust," excerpted below, John Davis and Robert McCormick provide two differing perspectives on the pope's culpability.

Robert McCormick argues that Pius XII's failure to publicly and forcefully condemn the Nazi atrocities enabled the Nazis to justify the evil they were committing against the Jews. He points out, moreover, that the pope's reluctance to speak out was engendered by his fear of Nazi reprisals not only against German Catholics, but also against the Vatican itself. McCormick argues, however, that the pope had many tools at his disposal to pressure Catholics to refrain from discrimination and murder. The first was the power of excommunication, which, according to McCormick, the pope never used. He states that Catholics were permitted to commit atrocities against the Jews without fear of retribution from the church. McCormick also argues that in claiming "Vatican neutrality," Pius XII thought he could then effectively negotiate a peaceful end to the war. In fact, he maintains that the pope's stance not only raised further moral questions, it reinforced the belief that discrimination against the Jews was acceptable, thereby permitting the horrific crimes against the Jews to continue.

John Davis, on the other hand, provides a different perspective. He suggests that in the person of Pius XII, the Jews had found their greatest ally. Forced to restrain his denunciation of Nazism in order to avert swift Nazi retaliation not only against the church but also against the Jews themselves, Pius XII worked covertly to save hundreds of thousands of Jews from the Holocaust. Before the war, the pope worked tirelessly to have Allied countries accept Jews who had been stripped of their rights by the Nazis. Despite the pope's pleas, few countries would take them. Nevertheless, Davis argues, the pope continued his pleas for help, while actively establishing ways, with aid of his bishops and representatives, for Jews to escape. When the war broke out, Davis claims it was the Vatican's neutral status in Nazi-occupied countries that enabled the pope to communicate secret orders to bishops, priests, and Vatican representatives throughout Europe, encouraging them to ease the burden of suffering Jews.

Robert McCormick is associated with the University of Carolina. John Davis is an independent scholar.

Part I: Pope Pius XII Did Not Do Enough to Protect the Jews, by Robert McCormick

At the end of World War II (1939–1945) Pope Pius XII, to all observers, was an emaciated, frail man. Throughout the war he had placed himself on limited rations and refused to heat the papal apartments. In some way, his self-imposed suffering was penance, perhaps for his near abandonment of European Jewry during World War II. As Pius was living the life of an aesthete, the Jewish population in Europe was being annihilated by the racial policies of Nazi Germany. Even with abundant proof of the Holocaust at hand, the Pope never uttered a clear and specific condemnation of Nazi atrocities. Little was done to support anti-Nazi forces and few words of succor were given to those Catholics who were hiding and protecting Jews. . . .

Pius XII could have been more vocal in condemning German persecution and could even have used the power of excommunication to pressure Catholics into refraining from anti-Semitic behavior and murder. His most powerful tool, excommunication, was never used as a threat for stopping the violence against European Jewry. However, he wished to be the key figure in preventing a war and, once it was under way, in forging a peace. Therefore, he steadfastly maintained Vatican neutrality, careful not to irritate the Nazis by condemning their actions. His ambition was to elevate the Church by triumphantly negotiating an end to World War II and thus raising the prestige of the Catholic faith in the eyes of the world.

Cardinal Eugenio Pacelli became Pope Pius XII on 2 March 1939. Rarely has a pontificate begun in a time of such great crisis. Pacelli, on the surface, seemed to be the right man for the job. He had extensive diplomatic experience, much of it in Germany, and enjoyed the respect of most in the Vatican. One of his crowning achievements had been negotiating and concluding a concordat with Nazi Germany in 1933. Pius had enjoyed his tenure in Germany and saw his successful negotiation of the concordat as a victory for Vatican diplomacy as well as evidence of his own political skills. Familiar with Germans, he believed that he could do business with Berlin. From his first day in the papacy until September 1939, he devoted himself to preventing the eruption of a European war. Failing in this endeavor, and presiding over Catholics in all the belligerent states, the Pope declared neutrality soon after the German assault on Poland. . . .

Failure of Leadership

Early in the war, Pius XII had opportunities to condemn genocides taking place in Poland and Croatia but chose to vacillate rather than denounce the holocausts occurring in these two states. Although never condemning German aggression or directly chastising the Nazis for their treatment of Jews in Poland, Pius noted the suffering of the Polish nation in the encyclical *Summi Pontificatus* issued on 20 October 1939. Little else was voiced until January 1940, when Vatican Radio reported that Polish Jews were being forced into ghettos where living conditions were perilous. This broadcast was the only direct reference to the suffering of the tens of thousands of Jews in Poland voiced publicly by the Vatican. Pius retreated from making any direct and specific appeals for more humane treatment allegedly out of fear of disaffecting German Catholics and concern that Berlin would assault the Vatican if he vocally condemned their activities.

In 1941 Pius XII had a second opportunity to denounce a genocide. Ante Pavelic, a devout Catholic and Croatian nationalist, established, under the auspices of Germany and Italy, the Independent State of Croatia on 10 April 1941. As early as May 1941, Pavelic and his Ustase (secret police) unleashed a genocide on Orthodox Serbs and Jews that ultimately claimed the lives of 450,000. The Vatican never denounced Pavelic's actions, preferring to look the other way since the new Croatia was destined to be a formally Catholic state. Pius and his advisers were willing to ignore Croatian concentration camps and murders because Pavelic's state was a fledgling concern that needed time to develop into a bulwark of Catholicism in the Balkans. His eyes remained fixed on the establishment of a Catholic state in the Balkans, blind to the heinous massacres perpetrated by the Ustase. Because Pavelic so eagerly sought Vatican diplomatic recognition and led a movement of zealous Catholics, Pius had the leverage to force Pavelic and the Ustase to stop murdering Serbs and Jews. The Vatican never attempted to use this leverage to prevent this genocide. Pius XII never condemned the destruction of the Serbian and Jewish population in Croatia, even though he held great sway over Pavelic and his followers. Instead, Pius met twice with Pavelic, a notorious murderer, during the war.

Ignoring the Suffering of Jews

Pius was well informed about the atrocities being conducted by the Nazis against the Jews. Beginning in 1941, an unending string of reports—all raising the same alarm—flowed into Rome from a variety of sources. Jews were being tortured and slaughtered. By December 1942, when information about the genocide against Jews was well known throughout the Western world, British and American representatives to the Holy See requested that the Vatican approve and join the Allies in a declaration condemning the Nazi genocide. Not only did the Holy See reject the Allied declaration, Harold Tittman, American assistant representative to the Vatican, reported that the Church believed that it had condemned atrocities in general, but that "the Holy See was unable to verify Allied reports as to the number of Jews exterminated." The alleged denunciation of atrocities was no more than vague comments in Pius XII's 1942 Christmas message. The language used, however, was so unspecific that even the keenest ears could not discern what Pius intended. In this rather weak condemnation, Pius never mentioned the words *Jew* or *Orthodox*, even though tens of thousands had been both systematically and unsystematically slaughtered.

The Vatican secretary of state, Cardinal Luigi Maglione, was not being forthcoming with Tittman, as it was quite clear through many reports in the media and from Vatican nuncios and others that thousands upon thousands of Jews were being sent to camps for extermination. What is evident is that the Vatican did not want to make any clear statement condemning German actions against the Jews out of fear that it would be construed as destroying Vatican neutrality and potentially unleash attack against the Vatican itself. As Myron Taylor, the U.S. representative to the Vatican, observed in 1942, the Pope was holding firm to neutrality at the expense of abandoning Christian morality.

There were several avenues that Pius could have taken to aid in mitigating the effects of the Holocaust. One such avenue was through his constant contact with cardinals and bishops throughout Europe. The Pope never issued clear instructions to cardinals and bishops explaining how to handle the Holocaust, although abundant opportunities to do so existed. Historian Michael Phayer has noted that in the Pope's many letters to Bishop Conrad Preysing, Cardinal Adolf Betram, and Cardinal Michael Faulhauber, "Pius never divulged to them the horrible news that the Vatican had learned in 1942 and confirmed in 1943, namely, that Germany had built extermination centers in occupied Poland where millions were being murdered." Rarely did he mention the suffering of Jews in any of his correspondence with them, although Preysing consistently asked for direction from Pius. The Pope intentionally avoided drawing attention to the Holocaust. He did not urge cardinals, bishops, or priests to pursue methods of protecting and saving Jews, preferring to let Catholics make their decisions independently. This policy was out of step with Catholic tradition and did not rally Catholics to the defense of Jews.

Papal restraint was caused by the Vatican's strong desire to stay neutral in the war, a fear of offending the German Catholic population, and a concern that any precise protest would engender worse treatment for Jews and Catholics. These justifications ring hollow when confronted with the reality of the Holocaust. Defenders of Pius often have noted that vocal opposition against the Nazis only engendered a worse form of retaliation. The case of converted Jews being rounded up in Holland after the archbishop of Utrecht condemned Nazi policies is usually cited as proof that Pius made the right decision to remain silent. But even when the war was entering its final stages and millions of Jews had been killed and millions more were being led to their deaths, he failed to assault Nazi atrocities. With German armies reeling in defeat, any statement denouncing Jewish massacres would have saved at least some lives. Even after Rome was liberated and the Pope no longer was concerned with the potential destruction of the city, the pontiff chose to make no direct statements against Nazi abuses. Pius could not bring himself to denounce the murder of Jews because he had become obsessed with the inexorable march of Soviet forces. To Pius, Germany was key to preventing a communist Europe; therefore, he preferred not to say anything that might weaken Germany, even when German resistance was faltering.

Pius Didn't Denounce Germany's Actions

Perhaps most telling of all was the pontiff's position during the arrest and deportation of Roman Jews in October 1943. Although approximately forty thousand Jews were hidden in monasteries, churches, and within the Vatican, more than one thousand were shipped off to Auschwitz. Remarkably, Pius never uttered a word denouncing German actions. German officials in Rome treated this silence as somewhat of a victory. German ambassador Ernst von Weizsacker, in a memo to the Wilhelmstrasse, happily reported that Pius "has not allowed himself to be drawn into any demonstrative statement against the deportation of the Jews of Rome." He even recognized that Pius's stance would raise the ire of the Western Allies. In German opinion, Pius was far from hostile to their policies. To the Allies it appeared that Pius was more interested in maintaining neutrality and remaining on good diplomatic terms with the Nazis than denouncing the Holocaust.

Some of Pius's defenders argue that he wielded little power to stop Nazi atrocities. One example contradicts this theory. Beginning in 1942, Bishop Kmetko of Nitra, with the support of the Vatican, strongly voiced protests against the deportation of Jews from Slovakia. These protests began to have an effect. Deportations slowed and then ceased temporarily. Catholic and Protestant opposition to the deportations convinced the majority of Slovaks that anti-Semitic attacks were wrong. This opposition had the effect of forcing the Nazi leadership to retreat from its wholesale attack on Slovak Jewry. Although deportations and executions resurfaced in 1944, it was clear that the Vatican could successfully use its influence to mitigate Jewish persecution in German satellite states.

Excommunication was never used against any Catholic who committed crimes against Jews. Never once did the Pope even threaten its use. Catholics were free to abuse and kill Jews without any sign that they would be held accountable for their actions. Even though Catholics comprised 43.1 percent of the German population in 1939, Pius refused to threaten excommunication. Although threat of excommunication did not carry the force of the past, it would have induced some Germans to reconsider their actions and perhaps have convinced others to protect Jews. . . .

Part II: Pope Pius XII Was a Great Ally to the Jews, by John Davis

Vatican actions to help Jews under Nazi rule from 1933 to 1945 were at once diplomatic and formal but also adroitly subtle and covert. In the end, the Vatican was the most successful government entity to act on behalf of Jews during the entire period.

This nuanced policy was rooted in the relationship of the Vatican with prewar Nazi Germany. The Vatican relentlessly emphasized racial equality while actively assisting Jewish emigration from increasing persecution. In addition, the wartime responses of the Vatican to the persecution and murder of Jews in various Axis countries, where dictatorial rule was by no means uniform, was as effective as it could have been under the circumstances. Once the Vatican realized that Jewish lives were at risk, that every method of intervention was a matter of life or death, it spared no effort to rescue them. As the papal nuncio to Turkey, Cardinal Angelo Roncalli, later

Pope John XXIII (who saved twenty thousand Jews in the Balkans), stated, "I simply carried out the Pope's orders, first and foremost to save human lives." By analyzing historical realities, one can establish how effective these policies were.

The Vatican represented a Roman Catholic Church that taught the common dignity and equality of man. This belief governed all its policy statements, initiatives, and actions. This fundamental tenet was the core conflict between the Vatican and the Nazi Reich. Repeated Vatican proclamations about the universal family of man flew in the face of Adolf Hitler's "scientific anti-Semitism." Every papal statement against Hitler's racial Darwinism, no matter how refined or oblique, was immediately understood by the adversary, as the Nazi secretary of state Ernst von Weizacker confirmed, "To be sure, the Vatican expresses itself in general terms, but it is perfectly clear who is meant."

One belief, universal and equal, could not coexist with the other, racial and supremacist. The church paid for its limited freedom of action by constant Nazi harassment, arrests, and executions of its priests. An SS document maintained, "A philosophy that assumes human equality . . . is an error or a conscious lie." The Vatican not only continued to present its ideas at every turn but also thereby laid the groundwork for all its subsequent actions on behalf of the Jews. . . .

Early Attempts to Stop the Nazis

With insights from the new science of psychology, the Nazis manipulated the German mentality. For example, Leni Riefenstahl's movie *Triumph of the Will* (1935) recorded Hitler's triumphant arrival at the Nazi Party congress as if he were a victorious Roman emperor. Hitler, filmed amid resounding music, klieg lights, and cheering soldiers shouting *Sieg Heil* (Hail Victory), embodied victories to come. A banner in every Nazi rally hall proclaimed, *Die Juden sind Unser Ungluck* (The Jews Are Our Misfortune). One leader with one goal demanded total submission. No other belief system could coexist with this exclusionary racism.

Cardinal Eugenio Pacelli, later Pius XII, identified this threat. Pacelli was the papal nuncio (ambassador) to the German kingdom of Bavaria from 1917 through the Weimar years (1919–1933). He saw firsthand the sufferings of the German people. He saw as well that Nazi victory would ruin the country. Philosophically, he was committed to the dignity of each person and understood that "the Church will never come to terms with Nazis as long as they persist in their racial philosophy." Together with Pope Pius XI, he carefully assessed the growing Nazi power. . . .

The Vatican reached a concordat with Germany in 1933. Within months the Nazis began to violate its principles. Whereas against the Jews the Nazis were harsh and overt, against the church the Nazis concocted outrageous allegations of sexual deviancy and financial irregularities among Catholic clergy and closed Catholic schools, institutes, and newspapers. The Nazis thus sought to undermine Catholic teaching authority and insidiously diminish Catholic ability to counter Nazi claims on anyone's behalf. In response, Cardinal Pacelli authored and Pius XI proclaimed the only encyclical ever written in the German language, *Mit Brennender Sorge* (With Burning Anguish). It denounced Nazi duplicity, as well as attempts to undermine agreed-upon rules and to usurp Catholic education. The Catholic position of the equality of mankind was restated. As when Pacelli clearly stated in 1935 to 250,000 pilgrims at Lourdes, France, "They are in reality only miserable plagiarists who dress up old errors with new tinsel. It does not make any difference whether they flock to banners of social revolution or . . . whether they are possessed by the superstition of race and blood cult," so again in the encyclical he wrote, "the enemies of the Church, who think their time has come, will see that their joy was premature, and they may close the grave they dug" and "whoever follows that so-called pre-Christian Germanic conception of a dark and impersonal destiny for the personal God . . . denies the Wisdom and Providence of God. . . . Neither is he a believer in God." . . .

Pope Pius' Efforts to Save the Jews

Upon his succession to the papacy in 1939, among Pius XII's first acts were the raising of an Asian, two Africans, and an Indian to the bishopric. The point was not lost on the Nazis, who closed churches and schools and arrested priests. His first encyclical, *Summi Pontificus*, again condemned racism, reminding that "there is neither Gentile nor Jew." It too was confiscated in Germany. While Hitler could proclaim his views to millions by the ingenious *Volksempfanger* (people's radio) he had mass-produced, the Germans were forbidden on pain of imprisonment, and later death, to listen to Vatican Radio.

Vatican policy in the prewar years was to assist German Jewish "emigration;" to help Jews escape the tightening Nazi noose. The Nazis stripped away Jewish rights with the Nuremberg Laws (1935). Jews were persecuted and expropriated; yet, no country would take them in large numbers as refugees, despite Vatican pleas and admonitions for help. Pius proposed to all ambassadors to the Vatican that their countries admit Jewish refugees. Small numbers were accepted. Pius even appealed to British authorities in Palestine. He proposed a peace conference to avoid war, but no major power agreed to come. He personally worked to have thousands of Jews admitted to Brazil. Then he appealed to all bishops to encourage their governments to help. Vatican emissaries throughout the world worked wherever they had influence to encourage nations to accept refugees. As with all the dozens of protests he formally filed as nuncio, he continued to denounce Nazi Jewish policy. The nuncio in Berlin, Archbishop Cesare Orsenigo, repeatedly intervened in Jewish cases. The Pope continually reemphasized the theme of the equality of man while he actively worked personally and through his nuncios and bishops on behalf of the persecuted. Alone amid governments who would not see or help, he struggled to find escape hatches for the persecuted, vilified scapegoats of Europe.

When World War II (1939–1945) broke out, Nazi themes changed. Now they claimed to be the last bulwark of civilization against Bolshevism. The Nazis saw the Jew behind the Red Menace.

The Vatican declared its neutrality. As neutrals the Vatican could continue to function with formal representatives in warring countries. It could, as in World War I, ensure that prisoners were identified and families notified. It rescued several thousand Jews stranded at sea and transferred them to encampments in southern Italy, where they survived the war. It could assure the movement of emergency food and communication between families, prisoners, and their native countries. It could file diplomatic protests against excesses where identified and privately argue individual cases. Above all, it could try to mediate among enemies and communicate diplomatic and other initiatives for those who could not. Indeed, the Vatican facilitated one German anti-Nazi scheme that foundered when the British refused to communicate, even through Vatican intermediaries. As Vatican peace initiatives failed, the fate of the Jews became ever more tenuous. . . .

The Vatican's wartime policy sought to prevent Jewish deportation to "the East." What was the ultimate destination of the Jews? Repeated formal complaints in Berlin merited nothing, neither by the Vatican, the Red Cross, nor any neutral entity. No power could halt these obsessive, ominous deportations, about which no appeal would be heard.

Pius intuited from the hideous treatment of the Jews in the ghettos and the transport stations that lives were at stake. He sent a secret letter, *Opere et Caritate* (By Work and Love), to the Catholic bishops of Europe. It commanded them to help those who "suffered racial discrimination at the hands of the Nazis," in any way that would save them. . . .

Pope's Personal Sacrifice

Pius gave secret orders to his nuncios to hide Jews in monasteries, to issue false baptismal certificates, to effect escapes, and to influence governments. They were to pay money; give medicine and food where possible; and establish homes, camps, false identities, even false functions for their suffering Jewish brethren. (Three hundred papal guards were disguised Jews!) Pius even spent his personal inheritance to save Jews being blackmailed by the Gestapo, not to mention hiding three thousand Jews in his private residence at Castel Gandolfo.

On and on the Vatican appealed, pleaded, cajoled, implored, and acted—openly, and secretly where necessary. Sometimes successful, often not, it was not for want of trying. Even up to February 1945, in Berlin, Archbishop Orsenigo sought to alleviate Jewish suffering. The nuncio in Bratislava was told to remain in place, in the ruins, so long as "some charity could be done."

Throughout the period of National Socialist rule, the Vatican intervened in any and every way that offered possible success in saving Jewish lives. In prewar Germany the Vatican fought on behalf of Jewish refugees. Formal concordats allowed the hierarchy to function, to influence, and to act to relieve the sufferings of Jews.

With the war, the Vatican remained neutral. This stance allowed it to function in occupied Europe, while nevertheless covertly helping the Jews, saving lives where possible. Absent the treaties, Pius could not continue to communicate with his representatives who understood the local conditions better, which allowed for fine-tuning a policy that had to be correct, since lives were at stake. Nuncios and bishops "on station" were in a better position to help in realistic ways and could remain on duty as representatives of a neutral government. Their actions, directed by Pius XII, were consistent, reminding the faithful that racism "was incompatible with the teachings of the Catholic Church." The hierarchy took any action it could to save Jews, be it hiding, forging documents, funding, assisting, or physically taking the defenseless away to safety. The Catholic principle of the common dignity of man provoked action, while Pius steered it. . . .

In the end, it is estimated that some 860,000 Jewish lives were saved by the actions of the Catholic Church. Of course, there is no standard whereby to judge the sufficiency of so many saved while so many died. Who, looking back, could not have hoped for more rescues? Certainly the Pope did, who watched his many efforts wax and wane. Yet, in light of all that was done, perhaps the Jewish proverb that he who saves a single life, saves the world, should suffice.

The Impact of the
Vatican II Council

John W. O'Malley

*John W. O'Malley is a Catholic priest and professor of church
history at Weston Jesuit School of Theology in Cambridge, Mas-
sachusetts. O'Malley has written many books, including* Trent
and All That: Renaming Catholicism in the Early Modern Era.
*In the following excerpt from his article, "The Style of Vatican
II," published in* America: The National Catholic Weekly *on
February 24, 2003, O'Malley examines the impact of the Second
Vatican Council. Convened by Pope John XXIII on October 11,
1962, the Second Vatican Council, or Vatican II, brought together church leaders from all over the world to update and reform church policy and practice. Church historians have noted
that despite the church's prominence and leadership in the world,
during the latter part of the twentieth century the Catholic
church, like the United States and other countries in the 1960s,
faced challenges to its teachings and authority. Vatican II was
the first council to initiate change from within the church itself.*

*O'Malley asserts that Vatican II instituted systemic changes
that radically altered church procedure and, more importantly,
how the church defined itself. First, Catholics were permitted to
attend Protestant church services such as funerals and weddings,
which was previously forbidden. Second, the Council's Decree of
Religious Liberty initiated a new era in which the church would
no longer seek to make Catholicism the "official" religion of every nation. Third, the church sought to redefine itself in terms of
its authority. According to O'Malley, the council sought to let go
of the church's uncompromising and authoritarian image, and
redefine itself as a church open to dialogue, solicitous of the*

opinions and ideas of others (both clergy and laity), and conscious of a greater need for mutual respect and understanding within the church hierarchy. The changes made by Vatican II, O'Malley asserts, constituted a fundamental break with the past. The consequences of these changes, he claims, were enormous. No longer were worshippers seen as docile "subject," but rather as active "participants" in the church.

Forty years have passed since the opening of the Second Vatican Council. To people born after about 1950, the council can seem as remote as the American Revolution. It is something they may have heard their parents or their grandparents talk about but not something that seems particularly relevant today. Even for the older generation, which can remember the excitement the council sparked and the high hopes (or deep fears) it engendered, the memory has become dim. Even dimmer is any thought that it might provide the blueprint we need in our present crisis.

I think the council provided precisely that blueprint. I also think that Vatican II intended to make some fundamental changes in the way the church operates and that those changes, should they be put into practice, would do much to address our current situation and give us confidence for the future. Perhaps the main reason they have not been put into practice is that the radical nature of the council has never been accepted or understood. Vatican II, for all its continuity with previous councils, was unique in many ways but nowhere more than in its call for an across-the-board change in church procedures or, better, in church style.

Reaction to the Council

Like many other scholars, I detect three major trends in the interpretation of the council. The first trend, a small one, sees the council as an aberration. The Holy Spirit was somehow asleep, at least during part of the council. The more moderate within this trend simply try to ignore Vatican II, as if it never happened. The second trend seems to be the largest today and can even be described as semi-official. The council, according to this group, made adjustments in the way we express some teachings and made some other changes, notably in the liturgy, but it did not make any significant break with the past. . . .

I belong to the third trend, which sees Vatican II as making a significant break with the past. . . .

Changes Implemented by the Council

If something of deep significance happened, what was it? What did the council do? What changes did it make? It is easy to list a few obvious things that marked a real departure from previous Catholic practice. Catholics could now pray with their Protestant neighbors, for example, and attend weddings and funerals in Protestant churches, practices absolutely forbidden before the council. Several years ago Pope John Paul II met with leaders of other faiths at Assisi and prayed with them. This would have been unthinkable before the council—a good example of "the end of the Counter-Reformation."

Previously, it would have been unthinkable in Catholic theology not to hold up the ideal that Catholicism should be established as the official religion of every nation, even the United States. The "Decree on Religious Liberty" changed all that, and in so doing marked "the end of the Constantinian era." The battles in the council over the decrees on ecumenism and religious liberty were fought not only with great passion but, especially by those opposed to them, almost as life-and-death issues. That minority, which was small but intelligent and fiercely loyal to the church, was utterly convinced that these decrees were changes so large that they could not be tolerated. In seeing them as changes of great magnitude, they were, in my opinion, absolutely correct, even though the wording of the documents gives little hint that the council had chosen to move the church along a remarkably new path. . . .

Vatican II was fundamentally about the church. That was its center of gravity. It did indeed ask and answer the basic "what" question: "What is the church?" To that question it gave traditional answers, although it distanced itself from the 19th-century answers, like "perfect society" and "essentially doctrinal society." It put special emphasis on the church as "the people of God." That emphasis was "new." But it really was not new, because until the Reformation the standard definition of the church in catechisms was "the congregation of Christian faithful governed and illumined by God our Lord," which makes the same point. The church is the Christians who make it up, no matter what their ecclesiastical status. There is a horizontal character to the emphasis these expressions indicate.

That character leads into the deeper question the council asked: "How is the church?" That is where Vatican II becomes radical—and where it becomes especially relevant to today. How is the church?—that is, what kind of procedures does it use; what kind of relationships does it foster among its members; what is its style as an institution?

Style? Is that really important? Indeed it is. The style of our nation is democratic. Without that style, there is no United States. What made Michelangelo a great painter was not what he painted but how he painted, his style. My "how," my "style" better expresses who I am than my "what." The "what" of John O'Malley—priest, historian and so forth—is important, but style is the expression of my deepest personality. "The style is the man." Style makes me who I am. "What kind of person is John O'Malley?" Kind and considerate, or cunning and contrived? That is a question about style. If I am loved, I'm loved for my how; and if I get to heaven, I will get there because of my how.

What, then, is the style of the church? The crucial question on people's minds today is not "What is the church?" It is about how we want it to be, how it is really supposed to be. How do we want it to be in its procedures as well as in the hopes and fears and loves of all its members? That was the big question Vatican II addressed and answered. It answered it by the specific vocabulary it used, which reflected and made explicit what the style implied.

What is it about the documents of Vatican II that make them unique in the history of the councils? It is their style. Is this not significant? Does it not call for comment? We all know that such a striking shift in language, the adoption of a new language game, shall we say, always indicates a profound shift in awareness and personality and cannot be dismissed as "merely" a change in style. We know, moreover, that content and mode of expression are inextricably intertwined, that there is no thought without expression, that expression is what style is all about. In dealing with style we are at the same time dealing with content.

A New Spirit of Openness and Dialogue

Style—no other aspect of Vatican II sets it off so impressively from all previous councils and thereby suggests its break with "business as usual." No other aspect so impressively indicates that a new mode of interpretation is required if we are to understand it and get at its "spirit." In dramatic fashion, the council abandoned for the most part the terse, technical, juridical and other punitive language of previous councils. Believe this, or else! Behave thus, or else! Unlike previous councils, Vatican II attached no penalties for failure to observe its directives, and it cannot be read as a treatise on crime and punishment, as can many former councils.

The style of the council was invitational. It was new for a council in that it replicated to a remarkable degree the style the Fathers of the Church used in their sermons, treatises and commentaries down to the advent of Scholasticism in the 13th century. The Scholastic style was essentially based on dialectics, the art of debate, the art of proving one's enemies wrong. But the style the council adopted was based, as was the style of the early Fathers for the most part, on rhetoric, the art of persuasion, the art of finding common ground. That is the art that will enable previously disagreeing parties to join in action for a common cause. The style was invitational in that it looked to motivation and called for conversion. It looked to winning assent to its teachings rather than imposing it.

I have just tried in a few words to characterize the general style of Vatican II. Let us now take a look at some specific vocabulary. The word dialogue recurs often in the documents of the council. After the council it was so shamelessly invoked as the panacea for all problems that it became painful to hear it. Even today it sounds "so 70's." That should not obscure for us the profound implications of the term. For the first time in history, official ecclesiastical documents promoted respectful listening as the preferred mode of proceeding, as a new ecclesiastical "way," a new ecclesiastical style. "Freedom of speech" is a value of the modern world, open to abuses as we know well, but nonetheless based on respect for conscience and for the dignity of each person's convictions. "Dialogue" tried to open the church to it.

The institutional correlate of dialogue is "collegiality." Collegiality means colleagueship. The term rests on a venerable theological and canonical heritage, but a heritage that since the 16th century had been consigned almost to oblivion. The term indicates collaboration between bishops and their priests, among bishops with the pope—collaboration, not just consultation. It indicates a break with the long-standing and then-current style of ecclesiastical dealing. Although the documents of Vatican II themselves give little evidence of it, we know from other sources that a change in the style by which the

Holy See itself functioned, especially in its dealings with bishops, was a special desideratum for most bishops who attended the council.

What was the style that needed changing, and whence did it spring? The style was "modern" in that it crystallized in the 19th century as the Catholic reaction to certain aspects of the Enlightenment that received their most effective and strident articulation in the battle cry of the French Revolution: "Liberty, Equality, and Fraternity." The battle cry overthrew the old order in Europe. As monarchies were toppled, so was their spouse, the church. Convents were sacked, churches desecrated, priests and nuns guillotined; blood ran in the streets. Godlessness seemed to triumph. . . .

A new papacy and a new papal style had come into being that emphasized, almost to the point of caricature, the authoritarian strains in the Catholic tradition and that set the church against and above almost every person and idea outside it. True, Benedict XV, Pius XI and Pius XII tempered these ideas and policies, yet basic elements of the style prevailed up to the eve of Vatican II.

This style ignored or badly minimized the horizontal traditions of Catholicism that had made the patristic and medieval church such vibrant and creative realities. Respect for conscience, with its deep, even pre-eminent roots in the Catholic tradition, had been badly sidelined at the very moment when it was being emphasized by secular and Protestant thinkers in the 19th and early 20th centuries.

It was a change in this closed, ghetto-like, secretive, condemnatory, authoritarian style that the council wanted to effect. If the council was "the end of the Counter-Reformation," it even more immediately wanted to be "the end of the 19th century," the end of the "long" 19th century that extended well into the 20th. The council did not want to change the church into a democracy, as its almost obsessively repeated affirmations of papal authority demonstrate beyond question.

But it did want to redefine how that authority (and all authority in the church) was to function, for instance, with a respect for conscience that transformed the members of the church from "subjects" into participants. This was a retrieval of that old principle of canon law: *quod omnes tangit ab omnibus approbetur* (what concerns everybody needs to be approved by everybody). Vatican II did not want the church to abdicate its privileged role as teacher of the Gospel, but it insisted that the church, like all good teachers, needed to learn as it taught.

The Invitation of the Council

To what, then, did Vatican II invite the church and each one of us? What is this new style? I think I can indicate its essentials in five points. First, the council called the church from what had been an almost exclusively vertical, top-down style of behavior to one that took more account of the horizontal traditions in Catholicism. This is most palpably manifested in the recurring use of horizontal words like "cooperation," "partnership" and "collaboration," which are true novelties in ecclesiastical documents. It receives its most potent expressions in the word "collegiality." The partnership and collaboration extend to relations between pope and bishops, bishops and priests, priests and parishioner—bishops and laity. In repeatedly describing the church as "the people of God" we see clearly the intrinsic relationship between style and content— between the "what" questions and the "how" questions.

Second, the council called the church to a style and mentality more consonant with serving than with controlling. One of the most amazing features of Vatican II is the redefinition it consistently interjects into the words "ruler" and "king," equating them with "servant." The pastoral implications are immense. To serve effectively means to be in touch with the needs of those being served, not supplying them with prefabricated solutions.

Third, nothing is perhaps more striking in the vocabulary of the council, nothing perhaps so much sets it off from previous councils as words like "development," "progress" and even "evolution." This is a sign of a break with the static framework of understanding doctrine, discipline and style of being characteristic of all previous councils. Vatican II never uses the word "change," but that is precisely what it is talking about regarding the church. What this implies, of course, is further change in the future. It suggests that its own provisions are somewhat open-ended. Whatever the interpretation and implementation of the council mean, they cannot mean taking the council's decisions as if they said, "thus far and not a step further." The council's style is thus oriented to the future and open to it.

Fourth, the council substituted for the traditional vocabulary of exclusion a vocabulary of inclusion. Instead of anathemas and excommunications, it is filled with friendship words like "sisters and brothers," and "men and women of good will." In this regard the handshake of friendship was extended not just to other Christians but to anybody wanting to work for a better world.

Fifth, the council moved from a vocabulary suggestive of passive acceptance to one that indicates active participation and engagement. The active participation of the whole congregation in the Mass was the fundamental and explicit aim of the reform of the liturgy. If the way we pray is a norm for the way we believe, may it not also be a norm for the way we behave? That is, may it be constitutive of our style as church?

The Catholic Church Seeks Dialogue with Other Christian Denominations

Paul VI

Pope John XXIII was elected in 1958. On October 11, 1962, he convened a council that brought together church leaders from all over the world to update and reform church policy and practice. This council was called the Second Vatican Council, or Vatican II. In assembling the council, John XXIII sought not only to modernize the church; he wanted desperately to reach out to other Christian denominations in a spirit of friendship and reconciliation. Of particular importance to the council was how the Catholic church saw itself in relation to other Christian denominations. Before Vatican II, Catholics saw themselves as part of the one true church, and other Christian denominations as lacking the essential truths that constitute the one true faith. John XXIII, however, died more than three years before the council ended.

Upon taking office, the newly elected pontiff, Pope Paul VI, continued John XXIII's call for change and renewal. In the next extract from the Decree on Ecumenism *proclaimed by Paul VI on November 21, 1964, the pope refers to non-Catholics as "separated brethren," signifying a fundamental shift in the perspective of the church toward its Christian brothers and sisters—a change, the pope argues, that was not only essential, but also in keeping with Christ's call for continuous reformation within the church. The pope maintains that the division among Christians has "scandalized" the world and undermined the spread of the Gospel. He argues, however, that although other Christian communities and churches are an important means whereby individuals*

Paul VI, "Decree on Ecumenism: Unitatis Redintegratio," November 21, 1964. www.vatican.va/archive/hist_councils/ii_vatican_council/documents/vatii_decree_19641121_unitatis-redintegratio_en.html. Reproduced by permission.

can attain salvation, the Catholic church is the only church through which one can achieve full salvation. He, therefore, encourages all Catholics to reach out to other Christian denominations so that ultimately they will embrace Catholicism.

The restoration of unity among all Christians is one of the principal concerns of the Second Vatican Council. Christ the Lord founded one Church and one Church only. However, many Christian communions present themselves to men as the true inheritors of Jesus Christ; all indeed profess to be followers of the Lord but differ in mind and go their different ways, as if Christ Himself were divided. Such division openly contradicts the will of Christ, scandalizes the world, and damages the holy cause of preaching the Gospel to every creature. . . .

In recent times more than ever before, He has been rousing divided Christians to remorse over their divisions and to a longing for unity. Everywhere large numbers have felt the impulse of this grace, and among our separated brethren also there increases from day to day the movement, fostered by the grace of the Holy Spirit, for the restoration of unity among all Christians. This movement toward unity is called "ecumenical." Those belong to it who invoke the Triune God and confess Jesus as Lord and Savior, doing this not merely as individuals but also as corporate bodies. For almost everyone regards the body in which he has heard the Gospel as his Church and indeed, God's Church. All however, though in different ways, long for the one visible Church of God, a Church truly universal and set forth into the world that the world may be converted to the Gospel and so be saved, to the glory of God.

The Sacred [Vatican] Council gladly notes all this. It has already declared its teaching on the Church, and now, moved by a desire for the restoration of unity among all the followers of Christ, it wishes to set before all Catholics the ways and means by which they too can respond to this grace and to this divine call.

Catholics and Ecumenism

What has revealed the love of God among us is that the Father has sent into the world His only-begotten Son, so that, being made man, He might by His redemption give new life to the entire human race and unify it. Before offering Himself up as a spotless victim upon the altar, Christ prayed to His Father for all who believe in Him: "that they all may be one; even as thou, Father, art in me, and I in thee, that they also may be one in us, so that the world may believe that thou has sent me". [Jn 17:21]. In His Church He instituted the wonderful sacrament of the Eucharist by which the unity of His Church is both signified and made a reality. He gave His followers a new commandment to love one another, and promised the Spirit, their Advocate, who, as Lord and life-giver, should remain with them forever. . . .

Even in the beginnings of this one and only Church of God there arose certain rifts, which the Apostles strongly condemned. But in subsequent centuries much more serious dissensions made their appearance and quite large communities came to be separated from full communion with the Catholic Church—for which, often enough, men of both sides were to blame. The children who are born into these Communities and who grow up believing in Christ cannot be accused of the sin involved in the separation, and the Catholic Church embraces upon them as brothers, with respect and affection. For men who believe in Christ and have been truly baptized are in communion with the Catholic Church even though this communion is imperfect. The differences that exist in varying degrees between them and the Catholic Church—whether in doctrine and sometimes in discipline, or concerning the structure of the Church—do indeed create many obstacles, sometimes serious ones, to full ecclesiastical communion. The ecumenical movement is striving to overcome these obstacles. But even in spite of them it remains true that all who have been justified by faith in Baptism are members of Christ's body, and have a right to be called Christian, and so are correctly accepted as brothers by the children of the Catholic Church.

Moreover, some and even very many of the significant elements and endowments which together go to build up and give life to the Church itself, can exist outside the visible boundaries of the Catholic Church: the written word of God; the life of grace; faith, hope and charity, with the other interior gifts of the Holy Spirit, and visible elements too. All of these, which come from Christ and lead back to Christ, belong by right to the one Church of Christ.

The Importance of Other Churches

The brethren divided from us also use many liturgical actions of the Christian religion. These most certainly can truly engender a life of grace in ways that vary according to the condition of each Church or Community. These liturgical actions must be regarded as capable of giving access to the community of salvation.

It follows that the separated Churches and Communities as such, though we believe them to be deficient in some respects, have been by no means deprived of significance and importance in the mystery of salvation. For the Spirit of Christ has not refrained from using them as means of salvation which derive their efficacy from the very fullness of grace and truth entrusted to the Church.

Nevertheless, our separated brethren, whether considered as individuals or as Communities and Churches, are not blessed with that unity which Jesus Christ wished to bestow on all those who through Him were born again into one body, and with Him quickened to newness of life—that unity which the Holy Scriptures and the ancient Tradition of the Church proclaim. For it is only through Christ's Catholic Church, which is "the all-embracing means of salvation," that they can benefit fully from the means of salvation. We believe that Our Lord entrusted all the blessings of the New Covenant to the apostolic college alone, of which Peter is the head, in order to establish the one Body of Christ on earth to which all should be fully incorporated who belong in any way to the people of God. This people of God, though still in its members liable to sin, is ever growing in Christ during its pilgrimage on earth, and is guided by God's gentle wisdom, according to His hidden designs, until it shall happily arrive at the fullness of eternal glory in the heavenly Jerusalem.

Today, in many parts of the world, under the inspiring grace of the Holy Spirit, many efforts are being made in prayer, word and action to attain that fullness of unity which Jesus Christ desires. The Sacred Council exhorts all the Catholic faithful to recognize the signs of the times and to take an active and intelligent part in the work of ecumenism.

Catholics Exhorted to Reach out to Other Christian Churches and Communities

The term "ecumenical movement" indicates the initiatives and activities planned and undertaken, according to the various needs of the Church and as opportunities offer, to promote Christian unity. These are: first, every effort to avoid expressions, judgments and actions which do not represent the condition of our separated brethren with truth and fairness and so make mutual relations with them more difficult; then, "dialogue" between competent experts from different Churches and Communities. At these meetings, which are organized in a religious spirit, each explains the teaching of his Communion in greater depth and brings out clearly its distinctive features. In such dialogue, everyone gains a truer knowledge and more just appreciation of the teaching and religious life of both Communions. In addition, the way is prepared for cooperation between them in the duties for the common good of humanity which are demanded by every Christian conscience; and, wherever this is allowed, there is prayer in common. Finally, all are led to examine their own faithfulness to Christ's will for the Church and accordingly to undertake with vigor the task of renewal and reform.

When such actions are undertaken prudently and patiently by the Catholic faithful, with the attentive guidance of their bishops, they promote justice and truth, concord and collaboration, as well as the spirit of brotherly love and unity. This is the way that, when the obstacles to perfect ecclesiastical communion have been gradually overcome, all Christians will at last, in a common celebration of the Eucharist, be gathered into the one and only Church in that unity which Christ bestowed on His Church from the beginning. We believe that this unity subsists in the Catholic Church as something she can never lose, and we hope that it will continue to increase until the end of time.

However, it is evident that, when individuals wish for full Catholic communion, their preparation and reconciliation is an undertaking which of its nature is distinct from ecumenical action. But there is no opposition between the two, since both proceed from the marvelous ways of God.

Renewal Begins Within Catholics Themselves

Catholics, in their ecumenical work, must assuredly be concerned for their separated brethren, praying for them, keeping them informed about the Church, making the first approaches toward them. But their primary duty is to make a careful and honest appraisal of whatever needs to be done or renewed in the Catholic household itself, in order that its life may bear witness more clearly and faithfully to the teachings and institutions which have come to it from Christ through the Apostles.

For although the Catholic Church has been endowed with all divinely revealed truth and with all means of grace, yet its members fail to live by them with all the fervor that they should, so that the radiance of the Church's image is less clear in the eyes of our separated brethren and of the world at large, and the growth of God's kingdom is delayed. All Catholics must therefore aim at Christian perfection and, each according to his station, play his part that the Church may daily be more purified and renewed. For the Church must bear in her own body the humility and dying of Jesus, against the day when Christ will present her to Himself in all her glory without spot or wrinkle.

All in the Church must preserve unity in essentials. But let all, according to the gifts they have received enjoy a proper freedom, in their various forms of spiritual life and discipline, in their different liturgical rites, and even in their theological elaborations of revealed truth. In all things let charity prevail. If they are true to this course of action, they will be giving ever better expression to the authentic catholicity and apostolicity of the Church.

On the other hand, Catholics must gladly acknowledge and esteem the truly Christian endowments from our common heritage which are to be found among our separated brethren. It is right and salutary to recognize the riches of Christ and virtuous works in the lives of others who are bearing witness to Christ, sometimes even to the shedding of their blood. For God is always wonderful in His works and worthy of all praise.

Nor should we forget that anything wrought by the grace of the Holy Spirit in the hearts of our separated brethren can be a help to our own edification. Whatever is truly Christian is never contrary to what genuinely belongs to the faith; indeed, it can always bring a deeper realization of the mystery of Christ and the Church.

Nevertheless, the divisions among Christians prevent the Church from attaining the fullness of catholicity proper to her, in those of her sons who, though attached to her by Baptism, are yet separated from full communion with her. Furthermore, the Church herself finds it more difficult to express in actual life her full catholicity in all her bearings.

This Sacred Council is gratified to note that the participation by the Catholic faithful in ecumenical work is growing daily. It commends this work to the bishops everywhere in the world to be vigorously stimulated by them and guided with prudence. . . .

Catholic Principles for Combined Services

It is a recognized custom for Catholics to have frequent recourse to that prayer for the unity of the Church which the Saviour Himself on the eve of His death so fervently appealed to His Father: "That they may all be one". Jn. 17,21.

In certain special circumstances, such as the prescribed prayers "for unity," and during ecumenical gatherings, it is allowable, indeed desirable that Catholics should join in prayer with their separated brethren. Such prayers in common are certainly an effective means of obtaining the grace of unity, and they are a true expression of the ties which still bind Catholics to their separated brethren. "For where two or three are gathered together in my name, there am I in the midst of them". Mt. 18,20.

Yet worship in common (communicatio in sacris) is not to be considered as a means to be used indiscriminately for the restoration of Christian unity. There are two main principles governing the practice of such common worship: first, the bearing witness to the unity of the Church, and second, the sharing in the means of grace. Witness to the unity of the Church very generally forbids common worship to Christians, but the grace to be had from it sometimes commends this practice. The course to be adopted, with due regard to all the circumstances of time, place, and persons, is to be decided by local episcopal authority, unless otherwise provided for by the Bishops' Conference according to its statutes, or by the Holy See.

We must get to know the outlook of our separated brethren. To achieve this purpose, study is of necessity required, and this must be pursued with a sense of realism and good will. Catholics, who already have a proper grounding, need to acquire a more adequate understanding of the respective doctrines of our separated brethren, their history, their spiritual and liturgical life, their religious psychology and general background. Most valuable for this purpose are meetings of the two sides—especially for discussion of theological problems— where each can treat with the other on an equal footing— provided that those who take part in them are truly competent and have the approval of the bishops. From such dialogue will emerge still more clearly what the situation of the Catholic Church really is. In this way too the outlook of our separated brethren will be better understood, and our own belief more aptly explained. . . .

Moreover, in ecumenical dialogue, Catholic theologians standing fast by the teaching of the Church and investigating the divine mysteries with the separated brethren must proceed with love for the truth, with charity, and with humility. When comparing doctrines with one another, they should remember that in Catholic doctrine there exists a "hierarchy" of truths, since they vary in their relation to the fundamental Christian faith. Thus the way will be opened by which through fraternal rivalry all will be stirred to a deeper understanding and a clearer presentation of the unfathomable riches of Christ.

The Church's Stand Against Artificial Contraception

Paul VI

Until the twentieth century, the Catholic church deemed that sexual intercourse between a husband and wife was for the sole purpose of procreation. The church taught that any attempt to prevent the procreation of children during the sexual act was morally wrong and against natural law. However, in 1962, the Second Vatican Council determined that the act of sexual intercourse constituted a core value to strengthening marriages and, as such, did not always have to be for the purpose of procreation. According to some Catholic theologians, the church began to acknowledge that the sexual relationship between married couples enhanced the marital bond. In addition, they determined that married couples not only have the "right" but the "duty" to determine the size of their families, in accordance with their circumstances.

In the 1960s Pope John XXIII convened a Birth Control Commission to examine the changes recommended by Vatican II. The commission's report suggested that sexual intercourse was designed by God for two distinct purposes; the first of which is to unite husbands and wives in a bond of mutual love and spirituality, and the second is to create children. In the commission's view, the use of birth control was therefore acceptable.

However, on July 25, 1968, Pope Paul VI published an encyclical (letters written by the pope to instruct the people) arguing that the commission's findings were inconclusive. The pope argued that the commission's members had not reached complete agreement with regard to their proposals and its moral intent, which, for the most part, was in conflict with the teachings of

Paul VI, "Humanae Vitae: Encyclical of Pope Paul VI on the Regulation of Birth," July 25, 1968. www.vatican.va/holy_father/paul_vi/encyclicals/documents/hf_pvi_enc_25071968_humanae-vitae-en.html. Reproduced by permission.

the church. *While the pope agreed with the commission's findings that sexual intercourse edified married couples and brought them closer together in mutual love, he concluded that the act itself could not exist at the exclusion of the greater act of procreation. In his encyclical, excerpted below, Paul VI argues that fundamental to the intimate union of a husband and wife is the intrinsic capability of that union to produce human life. Thus, despite the commission's findings, Paul VI's encyclical maintains the church's ban on "artificial" methods of contraception.*

The transmission of human life is a most serious role in which married people collaborate freely and responsibly with God the Creator. It has always been a source of great joy to them, even though it sometimes entails many difficulties and hardships.

The fulfillment of this duty has always posed problems to the conscience of married people, but the recent course of human society and the concomitant changes have provoked new questions. The Church cannot ignore these questions, for they concern matters intimately connected with the life and happiness of human beings. . . .

Commission's Report

The consciousness of the same responsibility induced Us to confirm and expand the commission set up by Our predecessor Pope John XXIII, of happy memory, in March, 1963. This commission included married couples as well as many experts in the various fields pertinent to these questions. Its task was to examine views and opinions concerning married life, and especially on the correct regulation of births; and it was also to provide the teaching authority of the Church with such evidence as would enable it to give an apt reply in this matter, which not only the faithful but also the rest of the world were waiting for.

When the evidence of the experts had been received, as well as the opinions and advice of a considerable number of

Our brethren in the episcopate—some of whom sent their views spontaneously, while others were requested by Us to do so—We were in a position to weigh with more precision all the aspects of this complex subject. Hence We are deeply grateful to all those concerned.

Response of the Church to Committee's Findings

However, the conclusions arrived at by the commission could not be considered by Us as definitive and absolutely certain, dispensing Us from the duty of examining personally this serious question. This was all the more necessary because, within the commission itself, there was not complete agreement concerning the moral norms to be proposed, and especially because certain approaches and criteria for a solution to this question had emerged which were at variance with the moral doctrine on marriage constantly taught by the magisterium of the Church.

Consequently, now that We have sifted carefully the evidence sent to Us and intently studied the whole matter, as well as prayed constantly to God, We, by virtue of the mandate entrusted to Us by Christ, intend to give Our reply to this series of grave questions.

Principles Governing Doctrine

The question of human procreation, like every other question which touches human life, involves more than the limited aspects specific to such disciplines as biology, psychology, demography or sociology. It is the whole man and the whole mission to which he is called that must be considered: both its natural, earthly aspects and its supernatural, eternal aspects. And since in the attempt to justify artificial methods of birth control many appeal to the demands of married love or of responsible parenthood, these two important realities of married life must be accurately defined and analyzed. This is what

We mean to do, with special reference to what the Second Vatican Council taught with the highest authority in its Pastoral Constitution on the Church in the World of Today.

Married love particularly reveals its true nature and nobility when we realize that it takes its origin from God, who "is love," the Father "from whom every family in heaven and on earth is named." [Eph. 3.15].

Marriage, then, is far from being the effect of chance or the result of the blind evolution of natural forces. It is in reality the wise and provident institution of God the Creator, whose purpose was to effect in man His loving design. As a consequence, husband and wife, through that mutual gift of themselves, which is specific and exclusive to them alone, develop that union of two persons in which they perfect one another, cooperating with God in the generation and rearing of new lives.

The marriage of those who have been baptized is, in addition, invested with the dignity of a sacramental sign of grace, for it represents the union of Christ and His Church.

Married Love

In the light of these facts the characteristic features and exigencies of married love are clearly indicated, and it is of the highest importance to evaluate them exactly.

This love is above all fully human, a compound of sense and spirit. It is not, then, merely a question of natural instinct or emotional drive. It is also, and above all, an act of the free will, whose trust is such that it is meant not only to survive the joys and sorrows of daily life, but also to grow, so that husband and wife become in a way one heart and one soul, and together attain their human fulfillment.

It is a love which is total—that very special form of personal friendship in which husband and wife generously share everything, allowing no unreasonable exceptions and not thinking solely of their own convenience. Whoever really loves his partner loves not only for what he receives, but loves that partner for the partner's own sake, content to be able to enrich the other with the gift of himself.

Married love is also faithful and exclusive of all other, and this until death. This is how husband and wife understood it on the day on which, fully aware of what they were doing, they freely vowed themselves to one another in marriage. Though this fidelity of husband and wife sometimes presents difficulties, no one has the right to assert that it is impossible; it is, on the contrary, always honorable and meritorious. The example of countless married couples proves not only that fidelity is in accord with the nature of marriage, but also that it is the source of profound and enduring happiness.

Finally, this love is fecund. It is not confined wholly to the loving interchange of husband and wife; it also contrives to go beyond this to bring new life into being. "Marriage and conjugal love are by their nature ordained toward the procreation and education of children. Children are really the supreme gift of marriage and contribute in the highest degree to their parents' welfare" [according to the Pastoral Constitution on the Church].

Obligations of Husband and Wife

Married love, therefore, requires of husband and wife the full awareness of their obligations in the matter of responsible parenthood, which today, rightly enough, is much insisted upon, but which at the same time should be rightly understood. Thus, we do well to consider responsible parenthood in the light of its varied legitimate and interrelated aspects.

With regard to the biological processes, responsible parenthood means an awareness of, and respect for, their proper functions. In the procreative faculty the human mind discerns biological laws that apply to the human person.

With regard to man's innate drives and emotions, responsible parenthood means that man's reason and will must exert control over them.

With regard to physical, economic, psychological and social conditions, responsible parenthood is exercised by those who prudently and generously decide to have more children, and by those who, for serious reasons and with due respect to moral precepts, decide not to have additional children for either a certain or an indefinite period of time.

Responsible parenthood, as we use the term here, has one further essential aspect of paramount importance. It concerns the objective moral order which was established by God, and of which a right conscience is the true interpreter. In a word, the exercise of responsible parenthood requires that husband and wife, keeping a right order of priorities, recognize their own duties toward God, themselves, their families and human society.

From this it follows that they are not free to act as they choose in the service of transmitting life, as if it were wholly up to them to decide what is the right course to follow. On the contrary, they are bound to ensure that what they do corresponds to the will of God the Creator. The very nature of marriage and its use makes His will clear, while the constant teaching of the Church spells it out.

New Life Naturally Follows from Sexual Intercourse

The sexual activity, in which husband and wife are intimately and chastely united with one another, through which human life is transmitted, is, as the recent Council recalled, "noble and worthy." [Vatican II] It does not, moreover, cease to be legitimate even when, for reasons independent of their will, it is foreseen to be infertile. For its natural adaptation to the expression and strengthening of the union of husband and wife is not thereby suppressed. The fact is, as experience shows, that new life is not the result of each and every act of sexual intercourse. God has wisely ordered laws of nature and the incidence of fertility in such a way that successive births are already naturally spaced through the inherent operation of these laws. The Church, nevertheless, in urging men to the observance of the precepts of the natural law, which it interprets by its constant doctrine, teaches that each and every marital act must of necessity retain its intrinsic relationship to the procreation of human life.

This particular doctrine, often expounded by the magisterium of the Church, is based on the inseparable connection, established by God, which man on his own initiative may not break, between the unitive significance and the procreative significance which are both inherent to the marriage act.

The reason is that the fundamental nature of the marriage act, while uniting husband and wife in the closest intimacy, also renders them capable of generating new life—and this as a result of laws written into the actual nature of man and of woman. And if each of these essential qualities, the unitive and the procreative, is preserved, the use of marriage fully retains its sense of true mutual love and its ordination to the supreme responsibility of parenthood to which man is called. We believe that our contemporaries are particularly capable of seeing that this teaching is in harmony with human reason.

Married Love and Procreation Is God's Design for Mankind

Men rightly observe that a conjugal act imposed on one's partner without regard to his or her condition or personal and reasonable wishes in the matter, is no true act of love, and therefore offends the moral order in its particular application to the intimate relationship of husband and wife. If they further reflect, they must also recognize that an act of mutual love which impairs the capacity to transmit life which God the Creator, through specific laws, has built into it, frustrates His design which constitutes the norm of marriage, and contradicts the will of the Author of life. Hence to use this divine gift while depriving it, even if only partially, of its meaning and purpose, is equally repugnant to the nature of man and of woman, and is consequently in opposition to the plan of God and His holy will. But to experience the gift of married love while respecting the laws of conception is to acknowledge that one is not the master of the sources of life but rather the minister of the design established by the Creator. Just as man does not have unlimited dominion over his body in general, so also, and with more particular reason, he has no such dominion over his specifically sexual faculties, for these are concerned by their very nature with the generation of life, of which God is the source. "Human life is sacred—all men must recognize that fact," Our predecessor Pope John XXIII recalled. "From its very inception it reveals the creating hand of God."

Artificial Contraception Is Intrinsically Unlawful

Therefore We base Our words on the first principles of a human and Christian doctrine of marriage when We are obliged once more to declare that the direct interruption of the generative process already begun and, above all, all direct abortion, even for therapeutic reasons, are to be absolutely excluded as lawful means of regulating the number of children. Equally to be condemned, as the magisterium of the Church has affirmed on many occasions, is direct sterilization, whether of the man or of the woman, whether permanent or temporary.

Similarly excluded is any action which either before, at the moment of, or after sexual intercourse, is specifically intended to prevent procreation—whether as an end or as a means.

Neither is it valid to argue, as a justification for sexual intercourse which is deliberately contraceptive, that a lesser evil is to be preferred to a greater one, or that such intercourse would merge with procreative acts of past and future to form a single entity, and so be qualified by exactly the same moral goodness as these. Though it is true that sometimes it is lawful to tolerate a lesser moral evil in order to avoid a greater evil or in order to promote a greater good, it is never lawful, even for the gravest reasons, to do evil that good may come of it—in other words, to intend directly something which of its very nature contradicts the moral order, and which must therefore be judged unworthy of man, even though the intention is to protect or promote the welfare of an individual, of a family or of society in general. Consequently, it is a serious error to think that a whole married life of otherwise normal relations can justify sexual intercourse which is deliberately contraceptive and so intrinsically wrong.

Pope John Paul II's Influence

Jonathan Kwitny

Jonathan Kwitny is a former front page feature writer for the Wall Street Journal. *Kwitny was also host of the PBS series* The Kwitny Report, *for which he won the George Polk award for best investigative reporting on television. Kwitny has also written several books, the most notable of which is* Man of the Century: The Life and Times of Pope John Paul II. *In "Book 4: Armageddon," excerpted below, Kwitny examines the demise of communism and the causes that contributed to its actual collapse. Kwitny argues that while President Ronald Reagan's "Star Wars" military buildup was important to the Soviet's demise, it was Pope John Paul II who was key in defeating communism. Kwitny cites many prominent leaders and government officials who state that it was John Paul II's commitment to nonviolence and his defense of the dignity and value of the human person, that struck at the heart of the Communist regime. As a young priest in Poland, the pope had provided the moral leadership to the Solidarity Movement, enabling Poles to face down their Communist leaders. Some world leaders, Kwitny writes, believe that it was John Paul II's election in 1978 as the first Polish pope that delivered the fatal blow to communism in Eastern Europe and the Soviet Union. Emboldened by his election, the people of Poland intensified their demonstrations, which led ultimately to the overthrow of the Polish Communist regime. Kwitny states that Polish efforts to overthrow communism became the catalyst for the eventual collapse of communism in other nations throughout Europe.*

What caused the collapse of communism? Those who consistently advocated violent tactics against it, and then saw it fall nonviolently, now credit *economic* violence. They say the "Star Wars" program and other parts of the Reagan military buildup led to the economic ruin of the Soviet system (though such intentions were specifically denied at the time of the buildup; Reagan justified it only on the ground that U.S. defenses were inferior). Referring to the buildup, one former Soviet official, apparently trying to flatter the Americans, said in 1993, "You accelerated our catastrophe by about five years."

Former National Security Adviser Robert McFarlane commented, "The American contribution to the collapse of Marxism was relatively small." Still, he contended, it was important. He said more money was saved by hastening communism's fall than was spent on "Star Wars" [a defense initiative].

Yet in all the debates and discussions that went on among Soviet policymakers—reflected in records that have become public of Politburo and Central Committee meetings—there is hardly mention of, let alone emphasis on, a race to catch up with Reagan's new weapons. A top general who proposed such an effort was fired for it in 1984. The Soviets had a long-standing problem of overcommitting resources to the military, a problem that burdened the United States as well. The Afghan commitment was an enormous drain, preceding Reagan. The increased firepower Reagan introduced in Afghanistan certainly caused more bloodshed, but there's no good evidence it altered the result.

From available evidence, the communist economic crisis of the 1980s was about the way the entire economy, domestic and military, was to be run. Poland and the other occupied states of Eastern Europe were in a similar economic bind, and *they* weren't trying to build a competitive "Star Wars" system.

Communist governments simply reached the rational conclusion that the only way to meet their needs was to reduce state command of their economies in favor of the marketplace law of supply and demand. Once cracks appeared in the communist facade, Solidarity [Polish Trade Union Federation] and its spinoffs in other countries were ready to jump in and pry the cracks wider until the facade shattered.

To a very large degree, however, Solidarity made its own cracks in that facade. When mass resistance grew in Poland in the last few years of the 1970s, hardly anyone—in Washington, in Moscow, or anywhere else—thought communism was in a terminal economic crisis. It was understood that communism generated economic misery, but that had been true for decades, and there was no reason short of KOR [Polish civil society group that emerged under Communist rule] and Solidarity to think it wouldn't continue for decades.

The Pope: Mightier than the Sword

Even when Solidarity was wresting actual control of Poland from the communists in 1986, few people recognized it as the last stage of communism. The economic crisis of communism was the egg to Solidarity's chicken: without either one—economic failure or the mass movement—the revolution probably would have fizzled.

One could also say that communism was doomed by technology. The arrival of the information age meant the end of mass industrial labor—Marx's proletarian class—in modern economies. "No class in history has ever risen faster than the blue-collar worker," the economist Peter Drucker has written, "and no class in history has ever fallen faster. In 1883, the year of Marx's death, 'proletarians' were still a minority." A century later, they had become a minority again, at least in the West.

Hand-held television cameras and satellite transmission also affected totalitarianism. It has been written that television ended the war in Vietnam by showing Americans the reality of combat; after that, its power only grew. An Auschwitz or a Gulag Archipelago couldn't be run effectively if television showed pictures of it every night. (Even in distant, fledgling Bosnia, pictures of killing eventually provoked Americans to action.)

One could say that if Solidarity had not come along to take advantage of these sweeping technological changes, something else would have. But Solidarity *did* come along—not anything else.

John Paul's longtime ally Bishop Bronislaw Dembowski says it is "unthinkable" that the pope would have accepted a military spending competition as a means to end communism.

Mieczyslaw Rakowski, the last communist prime minister of Poland, laughs out loud at the notion that Reagan's military strategy was decisive. "From the 1950s, the Soviet Union was under pressure to make our military force stronger because the Americans had new [weapons] systems," he says. "This competition was a mistake by the Soviet leaders. The reason the system failed was the flaw in the system. But the pope's influence was very important." He says Gorbachev talked constantly about the pope.

Father Avery Dulles, the theologian and son of the U.S. secretary of state who helped father the Cold War, says John Paul's role was "crucial. It wasn't the whole thing, but it was decisive. Poland was the key to the end. It influenced the other countries in Eastern Europe. Walesa [former Polish president who lead the anti-Communist movement in the 1980s] was on TV saying he never would have had the courage to act without the pope. Gorbachev said it."

"The Poles influenced everyone," says Vatican diplomat [Cardinal] Cassidy. "The Czechs and Romanians saw it, enough to make the point."

Mark Kramer, Director of the Harvard Project on Cold War Studies, says that based on declassified Soviet documents, Schweizer's and other books that credit U.S. policy for the collapse are "just plain wrong. The Reagan military policies were a background thing. Poland was of vastly greater importance. I've looked at hundreds of documents from the Politburo" showing debates about how to prevent civil unrest in the USSR "in response to the developments in Poland. In light of what was going on in Poland, they would send directives to local Party leaders to bring out consumer goods, improve working conditions, not have workers do unpaid Saturdays, to crack down very harshly on anyone who tried to start a protest organization. The threat posed by Poland was much more immediate and vivid."

Pope's Election Delivered Final Blow

Says Vatican spokesman Navarro-Valls, "The single fact of [John Paul's] election in 1978 changed everything. In Poland began everything. Not [in] East Germany or Czechoslovakia. Then the whole thing spread. Why in 1980 did they lead the way in Gdansk? Why did they decide, now or never? Only because they knew there was a Polish pope. He was in Chile and Pinochet was out. He was in Haiti and Duvalier was out. He was in the Philippines and Marcos was out. On many of those occasions, people would come here [to the Vatican] thanking the Holy Father for changing things."

Gorbachev [leader of Soviet Union from 1985–1991] himself (while not responding to my requests for an interview) wrote in 1992, "Everything that happened in Eastern Europe during these past few years would have been impossible without the pope, without the political role he was able to play. . . . *Perestroika* encompassed religion, a turnaround that culminated in the approval of the law on freedom of conscience. . . . This liberalization has a strong moral significance for all citizens, believers and nonbelievers. Today, even after the great change. . . . Pope John Paul II will have a leading political role. We are in a very delicate state of transition, in which the human being, the person, can and should have a really decisive weight."

Says Kazimierz Kakol, Poland's former communist minister for religious affairs, "The role of the Church was not [just] any role, it was the deciding role. The Church supported the illegal organization that became Solidarity. Without Wojtyla, there would have been no Solidarity and no defeat of communism. The [weakness of the] Soviet economy was not enough."

Christian Führer, a Lutheran pastor in Leipzig, East Germany, was inspired by events in Poland to organize demonstrations that helped bring down the Berlin Wall. He called it "unbelievable, that after fifty-seven years of . . . dictatorships the Christian spirit of nonviolence had come over the people, non-Christian as well as Christian. They turned to genuinely peaceful force and spilled no blood. In 1914, when all Germany was baptized . . . when the throne and the altar were one, the nation went to war. That, for me, was a blasphemy against God. And here, people who had never grown up as Christians behaved as if they had grown up on the Sermon on the Mount."

John Paul II himself told visiting Poles in the summer of 1989, "It is not an exaggeration when we say that it was Poland that resolved the gigantic dilemma of the division of Europe." He told a newspaper interviewer,

> I think that, if any role was decisive, it was that of Christianity . . . of its content, its religious and moral message, its fundamental defense of the human person and his rights. I have done nothing other than to mind and insist that this principle is to be observed.

Later, in his 1991 encyclical *Centesimus Annus*, he wrote:

> The fall of this . . . empire was accomplished almost everywhere by means of peaceful protest, using only the weapons of truth and justice. While Marxism held that only by exacerbating social conflicts was it possible to resolve them through violent confrontation, the protests that led to the collapse of Marxism tenaciously insisted on trying every av-

enue of negotiation, dialogue, and witness to the truth, appealing to the conscience of the adversary and seeking to reawaken in him a sense of shared human dignity.

It seemed that the European order resulting from the Second World War and sanctioned by the Yalta Agreements could be overturned only by another war. Instead, it has been overcome by the nonviolent commitment of people who, while always refusing to yield to the force of power, succeeded time after time in finding effective ways of bearing witness to the truth. This disarmed the adversary, since violence always needs to justify itself through deceit and to appear, however falsely, to be . . . responding to a threat posed by others.

To John Paul, the key to the victory was not the violent threat that had been marshaled but the violent threat that had been denied. His creed had won great contest. Now came a greater one.

CHAPTER 4

Contemporary Developments and Debates

Catholics, Abortion, and the Death Penalty

James D. Davidson

James D. Davidson is a professor of sociology at Purdue University. He has written several books, including Catholicism in Motion, Lay Ministers and Their Spiritual Practices, *and* The Search for Common Ground. *In addition, he writes a biweekly column for diocesan newspapers. In the following article published in the* National Catholic Reporter *on September 30, 2005, Davidson writes that based on a 2005 survey carried out by the journal, there is a discrepancy between what the Catholic Church teaches about abortion and the death penalty and how many American Catholics view these issues. Beginning in the first century, the Catholic Church taught that abortion is a moral evil. This teaching has not changed. In contrast the church's position on the death penalty is more complex. In cases where execution is an absolute necessity, the church does not oppose the use of the death penalty. However, if cases can be resolved nonviolently, then the church teaches that the death penalty should not be used. In his encyclical "Evangelium Vitae," Pope John Paul II concludes that the occasions "in which the execution of the offender is an absolute necessity 'are very rare, if not practically non-existent.'"*

Davidson claims that with regard to abortion, the gap between what the church teaches and what Catholics believe is expanding. In 2005, 58 percent of American Catholics believed that it was possible to be a good Catholic without agreeing with the church's condemnation of abortion. On the other hand, the per-

centage of American Catholics who oppose the death penalty is growing, resulting in greater support for the church's opposition to capital punishment.

Our 2005 survey shows that there continues to be a sizable gap between official church teachings about abortion and the death penalty and the way American Catholics view these life issues. In the case of abortion, the gap appears to be widening, while in the case of the death penalty, it seems to be narrowing. We also find little or no evidence of a consistent life ethic in Catholics' views about these life and death issues.

First, let me describe the context in which Catholics are formulating their views on these issues. I do this by reviewing abortion and death penalty trends since the 1970s, examining Americans' attitudes on the issues, and summarizing official church teachings. Then, I will turn to Catholics' attitudes.

U.S. Trends

Between 1973, when the Supreme Court handed down its landmark *Roe v. Wade* decision [legalizing abortion] and 2000, about 39 million abortions were performed in the U.S. (on average, 1.4 million per year). The number of abortions rose steadily from 745,000 in 1973 to about 1.6 million per year during the 1980s. Since reaching its peak at 1,609,000 in 1990, the number has declined to 1,313,000 in 2000. There were 16.3 abortions per 1,000 women between the ages of 15 and 44 in 1973. That figure increased to 29.3 in both 1980 and 1981. Since then, it has declined to 21.3 in 2000.

The number of death penalty cases in the United States peaked in the 1930s, when about 176 Americans were put to death each year. That number dropped steadily to 72 in the 1950s. There were only seven executions in 1965, one in 1966, and two in 1967, when executions were suspended while the courts considered their constitutionality. In 1972, the Supreme Court ruled that existing death penalty laws were unconstitutional. States responded by revising their laws to satisfy the Court. In 1976, the Supreme Court reviewed these changes and reinstated the death penalty.

The first execution after the moratorium occurred in 1977, when Gary Gilmore was put to death in Utah. There were no executions in 1978, and only two in 1979. The number increased steadily to a high of 98 in 1999. Since then, the trend line has been downward, from 85 in 2000, to 66 in 2001, 71 in 2002, 65 in 2003, and 59 in 2004.

Attitudes of Americans

Americans' attitudes about abortion have been quite stable since the 1970s. In the mid-1970s, 54–55 percent of Americans believed abortion "should be legal only under certain circumstances" (see the Sourcebook of Criminal Justice Statistics Online). Over the years, support for that view has fluctuated between 48 and 61 percent, with no overall trend.

Americans' views on the death penalty have been more volatile. Support for the death penalty declined in the 1950s and '60s, hitting a low of 42 percent in 1966. It rose during the 1980s and 1990s. By the mid-1990s, 75–80 percent of Americans supported it. Most recent polls show support has fallen to about 65 percent and that support for the alternative of life without parole is increasing.

Teachings of the Church

The church's opposition to abortion is clear and unconditional. According to the Catechism of the Catholic Church, "since the first century the church has affirmed the moral evil of every procured abortion. This teaching has not changed and remains unchangeable" (#2271). The church's view of capital punishment is more complicated. The "traditional teaching of the church does not exclude recourse to the death penalty, if this is the only possible way of effectively defending human lives against the unjust aggressor," but if "nonlethal means are sufficient to defend and protect people's safety from the aggressor, authority will limit itself to such means" (#2267). Alluding to recent advances in the forensic sciences, and referring to Pope John Paul II's encyclical *Evangelium Vitae*, the catechism states that "the cases in which the execution of the offender is an absolute necessity 'are very rare, if not practically non-existent'" (#2267).

Religion and Politics

There is a distinct gap between church teachings and American Catholics' views on these important issues. The percentage of Catholics saying that one can be a good Catholic without agreeing with the church on abortion has risen from only 39 percent in 1987 (the year of our first survey) to 58 percent in 2005. There also are striking generational differences among our 2005 respondents. Only 44 percent of pre-Vatican II Catholics say you can be a good Catholic without agreeing with the church's opposition to abortion. That figure rises to 56 percent among Vatican II Catholics, 59 percent among post-Vatican II Catholics, and 89 percent among Millennials. Clearly, Catholics do not feel as bound by the church's pro-life stance on abortion as they once did.

In *Religion and Politics in the United States*, political scientist Kenneth Wald shows that 55 to 65 percent of Catholics and mainline Protestants stress a woman's right to choose and 35–45 percent oppose abortion or believe it should be used under very limited conditions. Catholics and mainline Protestants are not as pro-life as evangelical and African-American Protestants, but they also are not as pro-choice as Jews and people with no religious preference.

Catholics also disagree with church teachings about the death penalty. A majority of Catholics support stiffer enforcement of the death penalty (54 percent in 1999, when we first asked this question, and 57 in 2005). However, our 2005 survey suggests that the gap between church teachings and

Catholics' attitudes on this issue might be narrowing. The largest generational difference on this question is between the three older generations (54 to 61 percent of whom approve of stiffer enforcement) and Millennials (only 41 percent of whom approve).

Are Catholics who take a pro-life position on abortion any more likely than other Catholics to take a pro-life position on the death penalty, as the seamless garment thesis suggests? If so, only slightly. Only 46 percent of Catholics who say one cannot be a good Catholic without opposing abortion and only 39 percent of those who say one can be a good Catholic without opposing abortion also oppose stiffer enforcement of the death penalty.

If there is any relationship between the two, some of the connection can be attributed to religious commitment. Weekly Mass attenders and people who pray on a daily basis are more pro-life on both issues than Catholics who go to church and pray less often. But socioeconomic and political factors also affect the way Catholics think about these issues. Older, southern Catholics who have a high school education or less and tend to be Republicans or Independents are most likely to be pro-life on the abortion issue. However, these conditions do not promote a pro-life view of the death penalty. Catholics who have a college education and are Democrats or Independents are most likely to be pro-life on the death penalty, but tend to be pro-choice on abortion.

Changing Views

In short, there is some decline in both the frequency of abortions and the use of the death penalty—findings that should please church leaders. Americans' attitudes about abortion have not changed much, but their support of the death penalty seems to be declining. There continues to be a gap between the church's opposition to abortion and Catholics' views on the subject, and that gap seems to be widening among young adults. We do not have any trend data showing a decline in Catholics' support for the death penalty, but generational differences suggest there might be some convergence between church teachings and Catholics' views on this issue. Prayer and Mass attendance foster a consistent life ethic, but socioeconomic and political influences do not. Catholics who are prolife on one issue find themselves in contexts that make it difficult for them to be pro-life on the other as well. The consistent life ethic is a compelling theological construct and religious commitment fosters it, at least to some degree. But, social, cultural and political influences make it difficult for lay people to embrace it in their daily lives.

The Sexual Abuse Scandal in the Catholic Church

Mitchell C. Pacwa

At the end of the twentieth century and into the twenty-first century, sexual abuse scandals within the church became high-profile news stories. The controversy first focused on Catholic priests accused of pedophilia. As more facts came to light, the investigations began to focus on bishops who permitted the sexual abuse to continue by simply transferring priests accused of abusing children to different parishes. In the following selection, Father Mitchell C. Pacwa argues that the priests' sexual abuse scandal has clearly engendered a crisis within the Catholic church.

Pacwa writes that the impact of the scandal on the Catholic church will depend on the manner in which it resolves these issues. He argues that the first duty of the church must be to protect children from additional sexual abuse, and that it has now adopted rigorous procedures for identifying and reporting sexual abuse cases to the authorities. Father Pacwa asserts, moreover, that while it is important that every care be given to protect children, it is also imperative that the church address the needs of those who perpetrate these crimes, whether through prayer or social and psychological counseling. He states that the church must never be dissuaded from ministering to the priests who committed abuse.

Pacwa is a Jesuit and a program host and producer for the Eternal Word Television Network (EWTN). He was formerly a

Mitchell C. Pacwa, "A Chill in the Church's Springtime: The Challenges Posed for Faithful Priests," in *Shaken by Scandals: Catholics Speak Out About Priests' Sexual Abuse*, ed. Paul Thigpen. Ann Arbor, MI: Charis, Servant Publications, 2002, pp. 115–22. Copyright © 2002 by Servant Publications. All rights reserved. Reproduced by permission of St. Anthony Messenger Press and Franciscan Communications. www.americancatholic.org.

professor of biblical studies and has written several books that include Catholics and the New Age *and* Father, Forgive Me, for I am Frustrated.

These days, faithful priests have to deal with considerable fallout from the sexual abuse committed by other priests and bishops. The lack of a satisfactory response from the hierarchy adds to the pain and confusion. . . .

Scandal Causes Embarrassment for Catholic Priests

Faithful priests face a number of difficulties in this difficult situation. First, they feel a horrible sense of dismay at such behavior by their own. When I was a boy, my heroes—Hopalong Cassidy, Gene Autry, and Roy Rogers—gave way in time (mostly, not entirely) to the young associate priests I knew, and even to the usually much-feared pastor. For most of us, priest heroes awakened our vocations at an early age and sustained our vocations during the long course of discernment and studies for the priesthood. We wanted to be like these good men who served God and neighbor unselfishly, men who were respected for their generosity, intelligence, and religious leadership.

The fact that brother priests—whom I still want to admire—would hurt the children I love and want to serve is thus an excruciating pain. No wonder so many of us feel embarrassment these days at appearing in public dressed in clerical clothes.

The great majority of our parishioners continue to respond to us with love for the priesthood and for those of us who serve our parishes. The people continue to attend Mass, greet us warmly, and frequently say, "Thank you for being a priest." I cannot be grateful enough for their support.

Priests Looked at with Distrust

While walking through malls or airports, however, the eyes of some people follow me, not with respect for the priesthood but with a look of suspicion. As I was boarding a plane recently, a woman standing near me, thinking it a joke, asked me, "Abused any kids today, Father?" I had not expected that, and I had no answer. She suddenly realized that her quip was not really funny, and she apologized as I continued down the walkway to the plane.

A priest friend of mine was shopping when another person said, "Shame, shame, shame!" as he waited at the checkout counter. He thought faster than I would have, and he asked to see her hand. Then he pointed out that even though all five appendages on her hand were fingers, not all were the size. She immediately grasped the analogy and apologized.

Sexual Abuse Scandal Jeopardizes Priests' Relationships with Children

A far more painful reality is the criticism of priests endured by the laity at school and work. Adolescents are not especially adept at making distinctions based on careful observation of facts. Children, especially boys, are often harassed by peers who consider all priests pedophiles. No priest wants his parishioners to experience such embarrassment over the sins of other members of the Church, so this becomes another source of pain over which there is little control.

Yet another problem is that many of us priests now feel self-conscious when we are with children. The vast majority of us, of course, have no desire to abuse young people. But suspicion of our desire to teach or show affection toward children has become a pollution in the ministerial environment. . . .

Healing for Both the Victim and the Perpetrators

At certain moments we priests certainly feel tremendously angry with the perpetrators of sexual abuse of children, but mostly we have concern for them. We may have been trained with them or by them; they may have been longtime friends with whom we took vacations; they may have been coworkers in a parish; they may even have heard our confessions or given us spiritual direction.

Furthermore, we know that we ourselves are sinners in various ways. Perhaps this particular sin seems more serious than ours, but we still want to have compassion on the abusers.

No doubt, on the one hand, our first duty—and the duty of the hierarchy—is to protect children from any further sexual abuse. Much more important than our embarrassment, anger, or disappointment is the safety of the children. We must do everything possible to prevent further crimes.

The victims have suffered a grave objective evil. The dignity of each one has been attacked. The emotional and moral growth of the victim has been thwarted. The innocence of the victim is disfigured. He or she can hope for and seek Christ's healing, but the optimal development toward healthy sexual integration within the context of deepest human dignity has been seriously damaged.

In light of this tragedy, the bishops and religious superiors have worked out guidelines and norms for reporting sexual abuse. We are now called to a new vigilance for the sake of the potential and actual victims. This entails a conversion of our own hearts to deeper insights into the dignity of each person who has been redeemed by Jesus Christ our Lord.

On the other hand, however, we must also consider the pastoral care of the perpetrators of these crimes. Men abuse children for a variety of reasons, reasons that are by no means fully understood. We cannot easily associate the problem with a particular background; the abusers come from all across the theological, philosophical, political, and cultural spectrums. Nevertheless, after establishing clear policies to protect the children, we need somehow to find ways to serve these broken men and their spiritual, psychological, and social needs.

Of course, many of them will end up in prison, but that does not prevent us from visiting them. Some will end up in psychiatric treatment. Most will become isolated from their parishes and brother priests. In that state, they will desperately need our help, and we must try to help them.

As a last resort, if they should refuse correction and conversion, we may have to treat them, as Jesus said, "as a Gentile and a tax collector" (Mt 18:17). He meant that we must treat them as we treat the unbelievers who are in need of conversion. They must become part of our mission, to the extent that this is possible.

This does not mean we must give these men so much time that we neglect our other duties. But it does mean that we must never cease praying for them, counseling them, and presenting them with the gospel of Jesus Christ. And we need not let our fear of scandal stop us from caring for these men any more than our Lord Jesus Christ was stopped from visiting the house of Matthew, where tax collectors and other sinners gathered.

Dealing with Priests' Sexuality

As priests, we have a double calling. On one hand, the Christian sexual ethic, based on the goodness of God's creation and its redemption from fallenness and sin by Jesus Christ, applies to us. No Christian is exempt from growing holy in the whole of life, including the area of sexuality. This is especially true within marriage, since the procreative and unitive elements of the sexual relationship exist within the holy context of matrimony. But single Christians as well must learn to grow in holiness and personal integrity.

We priests in the Roman rite, and many priests in the other rites, take vows of celibacy. Studies indicate that most priests appreciate the gift of celibacy and are happy within its demands. However, this general acceptance of the celibate state is still not without challenges, even for happy and peaceful celibates.

Though no priest may legitimately express his sexuality in genital ways, that does not mean that the issue of his sexuality is settled. Each priest must learn to integrate his sexuality into every aspect of his life. This includes dealing the right way with temptations and sexual sins, as well as enjoying the wonderful strengths of sexuality within the celibate life.

The healthy sublimation of sexuality into creative work and loving tenderness toward sinners is important. The integration of sexuality into prayer life—particularly through Confession, meditation, and self-knowledge—is a lifelong process. Just as other men go through stages in their psychological and sexual self-understanding, so do celibates. The joy is that the greater the integration of sexuality into the call to holiness, the greater the peace and effectiveness in the priest's life.

We priests need human support to accomplish such integration. Psychological insight is very useful, and consultation with psychological experts has helped many priests in the process of sexual integration. However, sexuality is not merely physical and psychological; it also requires a spiritual component, whether one is married or celibate. Also, psychology is frequently confused about sexuality, the spiritual life, and the meaning of human expression.

For these reasons, we need to seek out those psychologists who are capable of deep insight into the intricacies of sexual integration on a psychological level as well as a spiritual level. We priests can also help each other through our counseling, administration of the sacrament of Reconciliation, and friendships. We can offer each other support through struggles without slipping into a supportiveness for sexual misconduct. We can grow in that sexual integration which recognizes the respect due the sexual dimension of life and its influence on promoting one another's dignity before God our Creator and Redeemer.

In short, we priests can work through this present crisis and the sudden freeze it has brought us. On the other side is a springtime of hope for the Church. Our own souls and the souls in our care will be deeply affected by our approach to these problems, either for good or for bad. Let us endeavor to walk forward, confident in Christ Jesus that this is a wonderful springtime preparing for a new and glorious Christian millennium.

The Changing Role of Women in the Catholic Church

Mary Ann Glendon

Mary Ann Glendon is a professor of law at Harvard University. In her article "The Pope's New Feminism" Glendon describes the role of women in the Catholic church and argues that since the 1970s, the Catholic church has been a great ally for women in their quest for equality in the economic, social, and political realms—and even within the church itself.

Glendon states that during his reign Pope Paul II provided strong leadership in defending women's rights in the church. The pope made unprecedented changes that permitted "religious and lay women" to actively participate in all levels of the church. In 1995 the pope called for greater sensitivity and understanding among men with regard to the discrimination women have endured in the church. In addition, the pope increased the number of women appointees to pontifical councils and academies, she writes.

Despite these changes, the debate over whether the exclusion of women from the priesthood continues. Glendon argues that unlike other professions, the priesthood is not an occupation for which one applies. Rather, it is a calling placed on the hearts of men by God Himself. In other words, God chooses men to be priests—not the other way round. Despite this precedence, Glendon argues that this does not mean that women are not called to sanctity. On the contrary, she explains all people—both men and women—are called to holiness.

It was Vatican II that signaled a new awakening to women's concerns with a few cryptic statements, rich in implications. The Council spoke warmly of the idea that political and economic orders should extend the benefits of culture to everyone, aiding both women and men to develop their gifts in accordance with their innate dignity. In their "Closing Message," the Council fathers proclaimed: "The hour is coming, in fact has come, when the vocation of women is being acknowledged in its fullness, the hour in which women acquire in the world an influence, an effect and a power never hitherto achieved." . . .

Pope Paul II's Achievements

By the mid-1990s, it was clear that one of the great achievements of the papacy of John Paul II has been to give greatly increased life and vigor to the Second Vatican Council's fertile statements on women. In a remarkable series of writings, he has meditated more deeply than any of his predecessors on the roles of women and men in the light of the word of God. The vocabulary of these writings came as a surprise to many. Not only did the pope align himself with women's quest for freedom, he adopted much of the language of the women's movement, even calling for a "new feminism" in *Evangelium Vitae*. In his 1995 "World Day of Peace Message," he observed that, "When one looks at the great process of women's liberation," one sees that the journey has been a difficult one, with its "share of mistakes," but headed toward a better future for women. In *Mulieris Dignitatem* (1988), which contains the main theological basis for his messages to women, he labeled discrimination against women as sinful, and repeatedly emphasized that there is no place in the Christian vision for oppression of women.

The tone of all these writings is dialogical. Their author invites women to reflect and meditate with him about the quest for equality, freedom, and dignity in the light of the faith and in the context of a changing society where the Church and the faithful are faced with new and complex challenges. No one who reads these messages can fail to be impressed by the evident love, empathy, and respect John Paul II holds for womankind, nowhere more manifest than in his compassionate words to unwed mothers and women who have had abortions. The image that comes through is of a man who is comfortable with women, and who listens attentively to their deepest concerns. After meeting with the pope prior to the Beijing conference [in 1995], Secretary-General Gertrude Mongella told reporters, "If everyone thought as he does, perhaps we wouldn't need a women's conference."

The Church's Commitment to Women

Where women's changing roles are concerned, the pope's writings contain no trace of the dogmatism that often characterizes the rhetoric of organized feminism and cultural conservatives alike. He affirms the importance of biological sexual identity, but gives no comfort to those who believe men's and women's roles are forever fixed in a static pattern. On the contrary, he has applauded the assumption of new roles by women, and stressed the degree to which cultural conditioning has been an obstacle to women's advancement.

Despite the pope's statements, and the Church's unquestioned but often unappreciated role as a defender of women's interests in society, many women have felt that the Church has been slow to examine her own structures and the behavior of her own representatives in the light of the Holy Father's meditations. A glance at recent developments, however, shows that striking changes have occurred under his leadership. More importantly for the long run, he has provided a powerful set of guidelines for further and deeper transformations. Neither has the pope failed to confront past injustices and all the Rev. So & Sos throughout history: "And if objective blame [for obstacles to women's progress], especially in particular historical contexts, has belonged to not just a few members of the Church, for this I am truly sorry. May this regret be transformed, on the part of the whole Church into a renewed commitment of fidelity to the Gospel vision." Modeling this re-dedication to the Gospel vision in his own sphere, John Paul II has taken historic steps to raise the level of participation of religious and laywomen at all levels of the Church. In 1995 he appealed in strong terms to "all men in the Church to undergo, where necessary, a change of heart and to implement, as a demand of their faith, a positive vision of women. I ask them to become more and more aware of the disadvantages to which women, and especially girls, have been exposed and to see where the attitude of men, their lack of sensitivity or lack of responsibility may be at the root." He himself has made an unprecedented number of appointments of lay and religious women to pontifical councils and academies, providing an example for cardinals, bishops, and other priests throughout the world.

Obviously, one cannot expect the entire Church to be brought into conformity with the Gospel vision one year after the Beijing conference, or even thirty years after Vatican II. Cultural attitudes, custom, and sin are more stubborn than that. Progress will no doubt take place at different rates in different parts of the Church and her far-flung institutions. The journey will have its ups and downs, its false starts and blind alleys. Institutional change, after all, requires changes of mind and heart within individuals. As Pope Paul VI once said of the Roman curia, "It does no good to change faces if we don't change hearts." But it is already plain that a historic transformation is under way.

Diverse Roles for Women in the Church

Those who take a legalistic, formal approach to the study of institutions easily can underestimate the profundity of this process of change. An organization's formal rules often give a misleading picture of the actual status of women within the group. (One need only think of the United Nations as an example of an organization whose practice has fallen far short of its official commitment to sexual equality!) In the Catholic Church, a certain formal diversity in roles has in practice been accompanied by an extraordinary increase in female participation in the life of the Church since Vatican II. All over the world, lay and religious women currently are serving in many roles that were once confined mainly or exclusively to priests, men, and boys. Women are performing a variety of pastoral duties in parishes. They are swelling the ranks of missionaries. Perhaps not since the first century a.d. have women been so actively and visibly involved in the life of the people called together by Jesus Christ.

As for leadership roles, the Church's health-care system, the second largest in the world, is managed almost entirely by Catholic women executives. Catholic women, religious and lay, are superintendents, principals and trustees in the world's largest provider of private elementary and secondary education. (The Catholic Church long ago pioneered women's education, opening up opportunities for young women in countries where others paid little or no attention to girls' intellectual development.) The Catholic Church has no comparative need to apologize in this regard. . . .

The Controversy of the Male Priesthood

Given that the Church is in a period of such great vitality for women (and the laity), it is puzzling that some who purport to desire the advancement of women within the Church have focused particularly on the male priesthood. In most cases the explanation involves a confusion about the nature of the Church and the priesthood—leading to inapposite analogies from the secular realm. The Church is neither a business corporation nor a government. Its province is neither profit nor power, but the care of souls. Obviously, the Church cannot be run on the same principles as General Motors or city hall.

As for the priesthood, it is not a job, but a calling from God. It is not about power, but service. To be sure, this kind

161

of calling is reserved to men, but the call to holiness is universal. Who would claim that Mother Teresa's call to holiness is inferior to, because it is different from, that of the archbishop of Calcutta? Understanding of the ordination question has been further clouded, moreover, by a widespread failure to distinguish between the sacramental roles that are reserved to priests and the vastly broader range of pastoral and ministerial roles that can be performed by nonordained persons. Pastoral and ministerial roles today are more open than ever to women. Indeed, the Church in many places desperately needs and seeks the contributions of lay men and women in these areas.

Given that "the Church would just as soon canonize a woman as a man," and that so many crucial roles in the Church are not only open to women but going begging, why do some people continue to feel aggrieved by the male priesthood? As just mentioned, good-faith misunderstandings are regrettably common. In some cases, sad to report, the preoccupation with ordination has a darker side. The discussion at the 1995 conference of an American group founded in the 1970s to promote the cause of women's ordination is illustrative. It was painful to read in the *New York Times* that some women at that meeting argued that the goal of ordination should be abandoned, not because the Church had closed the question, but because, in the words of one divinity school professor, "ordination means sub-ordination to an elite, male-dominated, sacred, hierarchical order of domination." Others spoke in favor of persevering in the group's original aim, but the tone of their remarks was more anti-Church than pro-woman: "We need persons with chisels inside," said one religious sister, "chiseling away at that institution, or it's never going to come down." A professor of religious studies chimed in: "To ordain women is to give this rotten totalitarian system that the Roman Catholic Church has become the push into the grave." Needless to say, such sentiments are not shared by the great majority of American Catholic women, but they are given wide publicity by the media.

A Call for Understanding

Has the Churh done enough to conform its own structures to the principle that men and women are equal partners in the mystery of redemption? Of course not. Once again, Flannery O'Connor had it right. Forty years ago, when her proto-feminist friend railed against the Church's shortcomings, O'Connor replied, "what you actually seem to demand is that the Church put the kingdom of heaven on earth right here now." She continued:

> Christ was crucified on earth and the Church is crucified by all of us, by her members most particularly, because she is a church of sinners. Christ never said that the Church would be operated in a sinless or intelligent way, but that it would not teach error. This does not mean that each and every priest won't teach error, but that the whole Church speaking through the Pope will not teach error in matters of faith. The Church is founded on Peter who denied Christ three times and couldn't walk on the water by himself. You are expecting his successors to walk on the water.

In Support of
Same-Sex Marriage

Andrew Sullivan

Andrew Sullivan is an essayist for Time *magazine, a columnist for the* Sunday Times of London, *and senior editor at the* New Republic. *Sullivan is gay, conservative, and a practicing Roman Catholic. In the following essay, "What You Do," excerpted below, Sullivan opposes the Catholic teaching against same-sex marriage. The Catholic church teaches that homosexual unions do not constitute a marriage, since unions between people of the same gender cannot produce children. Sullivan contends that this argument is misleading and is used to discriminate against homosexuals for a condition they cannot change. He argues that there is no difference between an infertile heterosexual couple who cannot create a child, and a gay couple in a same-sex marriage. He states that it is wrong for the church to condemn homosexuality as "unnatural" while offering comfort, sympathy, and assurance to couples who cannot produce children.*

"Andrew, it's not who you are. It is what you do!" [politician Pat] Buchanan yelled across the table. We were engaged in a typically subtle "Crossfire" debate on same-gender marriage. I'd expected the explosion, but it nevertheless surprised me. Only minutes before, off the air, Buchanan had been cooing over my new haircut. But at least he could distinguish, like any good Jesuit, between the sin and the sinner. It was when his mind drifted to thoughts of homosexual copulation that his mood violently swung.

Okay, Pat, let's talk copulation. It isn't only me that has a problem here.

Buchanan's fundamental issue with "what homosexuals do" is that it's what he calls a "vice." (I'll leave aside the demeaning reduction of "what homosexuals do" to a sexual act.) Now, there's a clear meaning for a vice: it's something bad that a person freely chooses to do, like, say, steal. But Buchanan concedes that gay relations aren't quite like that; they are related to a deeper, "very powerful impulse," (his words) to commit them. So a homosexual is like a kleptomaniac who decides to steal. Kleptomania is itself an involuntary, blameless condition, hard to resist, but still repressible. Kleptomaniacs, in Buchanan's words, "have the capacity not to engage in those acts. They have free will."

Church's Teaching Against Same-Sex Marriage

So far, so persuasive. The question begged, of course, is why same-gender sexual acts are wrong in the first place. In the case of kleptomania it's a no-brainer: someone else is injured directly by your actions; they're robbed. But, in the case of homosexual acts, where two consenting adults are engaged in a private activity, it's not at all clear who the injured party is. Buchanan's concern with homosexual acts derives, of course, from the Roman Catholic Church. And the Church's teaching about homosexual sex is closely related to its teaching about the sinfulness of all sexual activity outside a loving, procreative Church marriage.

The sexual act, the Church affirms, must have two core elements: a "procreative" element, the willingness to be open to the creation of new life; and a "unitive" element, the intent to affirm a loving, faithful union. In this, the Church doesn't single out homosexuals for condemnation. The sin of gay sex is no more and no less sinful on these grounds than masturbation, extramarital sex, marital sex with contraception, heterosexual oral sex or, indeed, marital sex without love.

In some ways, of course, homosexual sex is *less* sinful. The heterosexual who chooses in marriage to use contraception, or who masturbates, is turning away from a viable alternative: a unitive, procreative sexual life. The homosexual has no such option; she is denied, because of something she cannot change, a sexual act which is both unitive and procreative. If a lesbian had sexual relations with a man, she could be procreative but not unitive, because she couldn't fully love him. And if she had sex with another woman, she could be unitive in her emotions but, because of biology, not procreative. So the lesbian is trapped by the Church's teaching, excluded from a loving relationship for no fault of her own; and doomed to a loveless life as a result.

Contradictions that Underlie the Church's Teachings

The Church urges compassion for such people (a teaching which, somewhere along the way, seems to have escaped Buchanan). But the Church's real compassion is reserved for another group of people who, like homosexuals, are unable, through no fault of their own, to have unitive and procreative sex: infertile heterosexuals. The Church expresses its compassion not by excluding these couples from the sacrament of marriage, but by including them. Sterile couples are allowed to marry in church and to have sex; so are couples in which the wife is post-menopausal. It's understood that such people have no choice in the matter; they may indeed long to have unitive and procreative sex; and to have children. They are just tragically unable, as the Church sees it, to experience the joy of a procreative married life.

The question, of course, is why doesn't this apply to homosexuals? In official teaching, the Church has conceded (Buchanan hedges on this point) that some homosexuals "are definitively such because of some kind of innate instinct or a pathological constitution judged to be incurable." They may want, with all the will in the world, to have a unitive and procreative relationship; they can even intend to be straight. But they can't and they aren't. So why aren't they allowed to express their love as humanely as they possibly can, along with the infertile and the elderly?

The theologians' best answer to this is simply circular. Marriage, they assert, is by definition between a man and a woman. When pressed further, they venture: well, sexual relations between two infertile heterosexuals could, by a miracle, yield a child. But, if it's a miracle you're counting on, why couldn't it happen to two gay people? Who is to put a limit on the power of God? Well, the Church counters, homosexuality isn't natural, it's an "objective disorder." But what is infertility if it isn't a disorder? The truth is, as the current doctrine now stands, the infertile are defined by love and compassion, while homosexuals are defined by loneliness and sin. The Church has no good case why this should be so.

Same-Sex Couples Stigmatized for Inability to Procreate

I harp on this issue of the infertile for one delicate reason: Patrick and Shelley Buchanan do not have kids. Why not? Generally, I wouldn't dream of bringing up such a question, but I am merely adhering to the same rules Buchanan has laid out for me. From the public absence of his children, as from the public statement of my homosexuality, I can infer certain things about Buchanan's "lifestyle." Either Buchanan is using contraception, in which case he is a hypocrite; or he or his wife is infertile, and he is, one assumes, engaging in non-procreative sex. Either way, I can see no good reason why his sexual life is any more sinful than mine.

Of course, by merely bringing up Buchanan's childlessness, I will be judged to have exceeded the bounds of legitimate debate. But why doesn't the same outrage attach to Buchanan for his fulminations against others whose inability to lead a procreative married life is equally involuntary? Of course, Buchanan goes even further: because of what he infers about my private sexual life, he would celebrate discrimination against me and use the bully pulpit of a campaign to defame me. Why is it unthinkable that someone should apply the same standards to him?

I'll tell you why it's unthinkable. No one should be singled out and stigmatized for something he cannot change, especially if that something is already a source of pain and struggle. Indeed, I would regard anyone's inability to have children, if he wanted to, to be a sadness I should privately sympathize with and publicly say nothing about. Why, I wonder, cannot Buchanan express the same compassion and fairness for me?

In Defense of Traditional Marriage

United States Conference of Catholic Bishops

The United States Conference of Catholic Bishops (USCCB) is an assembly of Catholic leaders in the United States and the U.S. Virgin Islands. At its annual meeting in Washington on September 9, 2003, the Administrative Committee, which is comprised of forty-seven bishops, including committee leaders and representatives of the fourteen USCCB regions in the United States, issued the following statement, entitled "Promote, Preserve, Protect Marriage." The bishops reaffirm that marriage is a union between one man and one woman and that it exists for the primary purpose of mutual affection and love, leading to the procreation of children. The bishops state that marriage is a sacrament, a sacred covenant that a husband and wife make with God and with each other. Marriage symbolizes God's greater love for his church and for his people. The bishops also argue that homosexual unions do not constitute a marriage, since unions between people of the same gender cannot produce children. They further believe that legalizing same-sex marriage undermines what they consider the nature and true purpose of marriage.

The Catholic Church believes and teaches that marriage is a faithful, exclusive, and lifelong union between one man and one woman, joined as husband and wife in an intimate partnership of life and love. Marriage exists so that the spouses might grow in mutual love and, by the generosity of their love, bring children into the world and serve life fully.

Moreover, we believe the natural institution of marriage has been blessed and elevated by Christ Jesus to the dignity of a sacrament. In this way, the love of husband and wife becomes a living image of the way in which the Lord personally loves his people and is united with them.

God is the author of marriage. It is both a relationship of persons and an institution in society. However, it is not just any relationship or simply another institution. We believe that, in the divine plan, marriage has its proper meaning and achieves its purposes.

Therefore, it is our duty as pastors and teachers—a responsibility we share with the Christian faithful and with all persons of good will—to promote, preserve, and protect marriage as it is willed by God, as generations have understood and lived it, and as it has served the common good of society.

To promote, preserve, and protect marriage today requires, among other things, that we advocate for legislative and public policy initiatives that define and support marriage as a unique, essential relationship and institution. At a time when family life is under significant stress, the principled defense of marriage is an urgent necessity to ensure the flourishing of persons, the well-being of children, and the common good of society.

Homosexual Unions

Our defense of marriage must focus primarily on the importance of marriage, not on homosexuality or other matters. The Church's teaching about the dignity of homosexual persons is clear. They must be accepted with respect, compassion and sensitivity. Our respect for them means we condemn all forms of unjust discrimination, harassment or abuse. Equally clear is the Church's teaching about the meaning of sexual relations and their place only within married life.

What are called "homosexual unions," because they do not express full human complementarity and because they are inherently non-procreative, cannot be given the status of marriage.

Recently, the Congregation for the Doctrine of the Faith issued a statement emphatically opposing the legalization of homosexual unions. Bishop Wilton D. Gregory, President of the U.S. Conference of Catholic Bishops, welcomed this statement and further articulated our own conviction that such "equivalence not only weakens the unique meaning of marriage; it also weakens the role of law itself by forcing the law to violate the truth of marriage and family life as the natural foundation of society and culture."

Call to Promote Marriage

We call on Catholics and other persons of good will to join with us in advancing this positive view of the importance of marriage for children and for society, and to defend these principles and the institution of marriage. This is especially important when popular culture, media and entertainment often undermine or ignore the essential role of marriage and promote equivalence between marriage and homosexual relationships.

We will do this in our teaching and preaching, but also in our public policy advocacy at the state and national levels and in the important dialogue about how best to protect marriage and the common good in the U.S. Constitution and in our society as a whole. We offer general support for a Federal Marriage Amendment to the U.S. Constitution as we continue to work to protect marriage in state legislatures, the courts, the Congress and other appropriate forums.

Thus, we strongly oppose any legislative and judicial attempts, both at state and federal levels, to grant same-sex unions the equivalent status and rights of marriage—by naming them marriage, civil unions or by other means.

Appendix

LIST OF POPES

1. St. Peter (32–67)
2. St. Linus (67–76)
3. St. Anacletus (Cletus) (76–88)
4. St. Clement I (88–97)
5. St. Evaristus (97–105)
6. St. Alexander I (105–115)
7. St. Sixtus I (115–125)—also called Xystus I
8. St. Telesphorus (125–136)
9. St. Hyginus (136–140)
10. St. Pius I (140–155)
11. St. Anicetus (155–166)
12. St. Soter (166–175)
13. St. Eleutherius (175–189)
14. St. Victor I (189–199)
15. St. Zephyrinus (199–217)
16. St. Callistus I (217–22)
17. St. Urban I (222–30)
18. St. Pontain (230–35)
19. St. Anterus (235–36)
20. St. Fabian (236–50)
21. St. Cornelius (251–53)
22. St. Lucius I (253–54)
23. St. Stephen I (254–257)
24. St. Sixtus II (257–258)
25. St. Dionysius (260–268)

26. St. Felix I (269–274)
27. St. Eutychian (275–283)
28. St. Caius (283–296)—also called Gaius
29. St. Marcellinus (296–304)
30. St. Marcellus I (308–309)
31. St. Eusebius (309 or 310)
32. St. Miltiades (311–14)
33. St. Sylvester I (314–35)
34. St. Marcus (336)
35. St. Julius I (337–52)
36. Liberius (352–66)
37. St. Damasus I (366–83)
38. St. Siricius (384–99)
39. St. Anastasius I (399–401)
40. St. Innocent I (401–17)
41. St. Zosimus (417–18)
42. St. Boniface I (418–22)
43. St. Celestine I (422–32)
44. St. Sixtus III (432–40)
45. St. Leo I (the Great) (440–61)
46. St. Hilarius (461–68)
47. St. Simplicius (468–83)
48. St. Felix III (II) (483–92)
49. St. Gelasius I (492–96)
50. Anastasius II (496–98)
51. St. Symmachus (498–514)
52. St. Hormisdas (514–23)
53. St. John I (523–26)
54. St. Felix IV (III) (526–30)
55. Boniface II (530–32)

56. John II (533–35)
57. St. Agapetus I (535–36)—also called Agapitus I
58. St. Silverius (536–37)
59. Vigilius (537–55)
60. Pelagius I (556–61)
61. John III (561–74)
62. Benedict I (575–79)
63. Pelagius II (579–90)
64. St. Gregory I (the Great) (590–604)
65. Sabinian (604–606)
66. Boniface III (607)
67. St. Boniface IV (608–15)
68. St. Deusdedit (Adeodatus I) (615–18)
69. Boniface V (619–25)
70. Honorius I (625–38)
71. Severinus (640)
72. John IV (640–42)
73. Theodore I (642–49)
74. St. Martin I (649–55)
75. St. Eugene I (655–57)
76. St. Vitalian (657–72)
77. Adeodatus (II) (672–76)
78. Donus (676–78)
79. St. Agatho (678–81)
80. St. Leo II (682–83)
81. St. Benedict II (684–85)
82. John V (685–86)
83. Conon (686–87)
84. St. Sergius I (687–701)
85. John VI (701–05)

86. John VII (705–07)

87. Sisinnius (708)

88. Constantine (708–15)

89. St. Gregory II (715–31)

90. St. Gregory III (731–41)

91. St. Zachary (741–52)

92. Stephen II (752)—*Because he died before being consecrated, some lists (including the Vatican's official list) omit him.*

93. Stephen III (752–57)

94. St. Paul I (757–67)

95. Stephen IV (767–72)

96. Adrian I (772–95)

97. St. Leo III (795–816)

98. Stephen V (816–17)

99. St. Paschal I (817–24)

100. Eugene II (824–27)

101. Valentine (827)

102. Gregory IV (827–44)

103. Sergius II (844–47)

104. St. Leo IV (847–55)

105. Benedict III (855–58)

106. St. Nicholas I (the Great) (858–67)

107. Adrian II (867–72)

108. John VIII (872–82)

109. Marinus I (882–84)

110. St. Adrian III (884–85)

111. Stephen VI (885–91)

112. Formosus (891–96)

113. Boniface VI (896)

114. Stephen VII (896–97)
115. Romanus (897)
116. Theodore II (897)
117. John IX (898–900)
118. Benedict IV (900–03)
119. Leo V (903)
120. Sergius III (904–11)
121. Anastasius III (911–13)
122. Lando (913–14)
123. John X (914–28)
124. Leo VI (928)
125. Stephen VIII (929–31)
126. John XI (931–35)
127. Leo VII (936–39)
128. Stephen IX (939–42)
129. Marinus II (942–46)
130. Agapetus II (946–55)
131. John XII (955–63)
132. Leo VIII (963–64)
133. Benedict V (964)
134. John XIII (965–72)
135. Benedict VI (973–74)
136. Benedict VII (974–83)
137. John XIV (983–84)
138. John XV (985–96)
139. Gregory V (996–99)
140. Sylvester II (999–1003)
141. John XVII (1003)
142. John XVIII (1003–09)
143. Sergius IV (1009–12)

144. Benedict VIII (1012–24)

145. John XIX (1024–32)

146. Benedict IX (1032–45)

147. Sylvester III (1045)—*Considered by some to be an antipope*

148. Benedict IX (1045)

149. Gregory VI (1045–46)

150. Clement II (1046–47)

151. Benedict IX (1047–48)

152. Damasus II (1048)

153. St. Leo IX (1049–54)

154. Victor II (1055–57)

155. Stephen X (1057–58)

156. Nicholas II (1058–61)

157. Alexander II (1061–73)

158. St. Gregory VII (1073–85)

159. Blessed Victor III (1086–87)

160. Blessed Urban II (1088–99)

161. Paschal II (1099–1118)

162. Gelasius II (1118–19)

163. Callistus II (1119–24)

164. Honorius II (1124–30)

165. Innocent II (1130–43)

166. Celestine II (1143–44)

167. Lucius II (1144–45)

168. Blessed Eugene III (1145–53)

169. Anastasius IV (1153–54)

170. Adrian IV (1154–59)

171. Alexander III (1159–81)

172. Lucius III (1181–85)

173. Urban III (1185–87)
174. Gregory VIII (1187)
175. Clement III (1187–91)
176. Celestine III (1191–98)
177. Innocent III (1198–1216)
178. Honorius III (1216–27)
179. Gregory IX (1227–41)
180. Celestine IV (1241)
181. Innocent IV (1243–54)
182. Alexander IV (1254–61)
183. Urban IV (1261–64)
184. Clement IV (1265–68)
185. Blessed Gregory X (1271–76)
186. Blessed Innocent V (1276)
187. Adrian V (1276)
188. John XXI (1276–77)
189. Nicholas III (1277–80)
190. Martin IV (1281–85)
191. Honorius IV (1285–87)
192. Nicholas IV (1288–92)
193. St. Celestine V (1294)
194. Boniface VIII (1294–1303)
195. Blessed Benedict XI (1303–04)
196. Clement V (1305–14)
197. John XXII (1316–34)
198. Benedict XII (1334–42)
199. Clement VI (1342–52)
200. Innocent VI (1352–62)
201. Blessed Urban V (1362–70)
202. Gregory XI (1370–78)

203. Urban VI (1378–89)

204. Boniface IX (1389–1404)

205. Innocent VII (1404–06)

206. Gregory XII (1406–15)

207. Martin V (1417–31)

208. Eugene IV (1431–47)

209. Nicholas V (1447–55)

210. Callistus III (1455–58)

211. Pius II (1458–64)

212. Paul II (1464–71)

213. Sixtus IV (1471–84)

214. Innocent VIII (1484–92)

215. Alexander VI (1492–1503)

216. Pius III (1503)

217. Julius II (1503–13)

218. Leo X (1513–21)

219. Adrian VI (1522–23)

220. Clement VII (1523–34)

221. Paul III (1534–49)

222. Julius III (1550–55)

223. Marcellus II (1555)

224. Paul IV (1555–59)

225. Pius IV (1559–65)

226. St. Pius V (1566–72)

227. Gregory XIII (1572–85)

228. Sixtus V (1585–90)

229. Urban VII (1590)

230. Gregory XIV (1590–91)

231. Innocent IX (1591)

232. Clement VIII (1592–1605)

233. Leo XI (1605)

234. Paul V (1605–21)

235. Gregory XV (1621–23)

236. Urban VIII (1623–44)

237. Innocent X (1644–55)

238. Alexander VII (1655–67)

239. Clement IX (1667–69)

240. Clement X (1670–76)

241. Blessed Innocent XI (1676–89)

242. Alexander VIII (1689–91)

243. Innocent XII (1691–1700)

244. Clement XI (1700–21)

245. Innocent XIII (1721–24)

246. Benedict XIII (1724–30)

247. Clement XII (1730–40)

248. Benedict XIV (1740–58)

249. Clement XIII (1758–69)

250. Clement XIV (1769–74)

251. Pius VI (1775–99)

252. Pius VII (1800–23)

253. Leo XII (1823–29)

254. Pius VIII (1829–30)

255. Gregory XVI (1831–46)

256. Blessed Pius IX (1846–78)

257. Leo XIII (1878–1903)

258. St. Pius X (1903–14)

259. Benedict XV (1914–22)

260. Pius XI (1922–39)

261. Pius XII (1939–58)

262. Blessed John XXIII (1958–63)

263. Paul VI (1963–78)
264. John Paul I (1978)
265. John Paul II (1978–2005)
266. Benedict XVI (2005–)

Chronology

1

Jesus of Nazareth is born in the town of Bethlehem.

33

Jesus is crucified by the Roman Empire and resurrected.

35

Paul converts to Christianity.

46

Paul begins missionary journeys.

50

The Council of Jerusalem frees Gentile believers from Jewish law.

57

Paul writes his letter to the Romans.

64

The fire of Rome occurs; the emperor Nero blames Christians and launches persecutions of them.

70

Titus and his Roman army destroy Jerusalem.

312

Constantine converts to Christianity.

313

The Edict of Milan changes Christianity from a persecuted sect to a tolerated religion.

325

The Council of Nicea approves the idea that Jesus is fully God.

386

Augustine converts to Christianity.

405

Jerome completes the Vulgate, his Latin translation of the Bible.

432

Patrick begins his mission to convert the Irish.

496

Clovis I, pagan King of the Franks, converts to the Catholic faith.

711

Muslim armies invade Spain.

732

Muslim advance into Western Europe halted by Charles Martel at Poitiers, France.

800

King Charlemagne of the Franks is crowned Holy Roman Emperor in the West by Pope Leo III.

910

Great Benedictine monastery of Cluny rejuvenates western monasticism. Monasteries spread throughout the isolated regions of Western Europe.

988

Russia converts to the Eastern Orthodox faith.

1099

Recapture of Jerusalem by the First Crusade.

1054

The Great Schism occurs, in which the eastern and western churches split.

1095

The First Crusade is launched.

1205

Saint Francis of Assisi becomes a hermit, founding the Franciscan order of friars.

1272

Thomas Aquinas finishes his *Summa Theologiae.*

1305

French influence causes the pope to move from Rome to Avignon.

1453

Constantinople falls to Islam, marking the end of the Eastern Roman Empire.

1456

Johannes Gutenberg produces the first printed Bible.

1517

Martin Luther posts his Ninety-five Theses.

1525

The Anabaptist movement starts, making the Reformation more radical.

1534

England breaks away from the Catholic church and creates the Anglican church.

1536

John Calvin writes the first edition of his *Institute of the Christian Religion.*

1540

Ignatius of Loyola gains approval for the Society of Jesus (the Jesuits).

1545

The Council of Trent is convened.

1563

John Foxe's *Book of Martyrs* is published.

1577

Teresa of Avila writes *The Interior Castle*, one of the classic works of Catholic mysticism.

1611

The King James version of the Bible is published.

1685

Louis XIV revokes the Edict of Nantes in hopes of gaining papal favor.

1769

Junípero Serra establishes Mission San Diego de Alcala, the first of the Spanish.

1870

First Vatican Council issues the dogma of papal infallibility.

1929

The Lateran treaties establish an independent Vatican City.

1939

World War II begins in Europe. The Vatican declares neutrality.

1944

The German Army occupies Rome.

1950

The Assumption of Mary is declared as dogma.

1962

The Second Vatican Council is convened.

1978

Pope John Paul II becomes the first non-Italian pope in 450 years.

2002

Former priest John Geoghan is convicted of child molestation and sentenced to ten years in prison.

April 2, 2005

Pope John Paul II dies at the age of 84.

April 19, 2005

German-born Cardinal Joseph Ratzinger is elected by the College of Cardinals as Pope Benedict XVI.

For Further Research

Encyclopedias, Catechisms, and Manuscripts

Matthew Bunson, ed., *2003 Our Sunday Visitor's Catholic Almanac*. Huntington, IN: Our Sunday Visitor, 2002.

Catechism of the Catholic Church. Washington, D.C.: United States Catholic Conference, 2nd edition, 2000.

The Companion to the Catechism of the Catholic Church. San Francisco: Ignatius Press, 1994.

Austin P. Flannery, ed., *Vatican Council II: Volume 2: The Conciliar & Post Conciliar Documents*. Collegeville, MN: Liturgical Press, 1998.

Michael Glazier and Thomas J. Shelley, eds., *The Encyclopedia of American Catholic History*. Collegeville, MN: Liturgical Press, 1997.

Michael Glazier and Monika K. Hellwig, *The Modern Catholic Encyclopedia*. Collegeville, MN: Liturgical Press, 1994.

Richard P. McBrien, *Catholicism: New Study*. San Francisco: Harper San Francisco, 1994.

Richard P. McBrien, ed., *The HarperCollins Encyclopedia of Catholicism*. San Francisco: Harper San Francisco, 1995.

New Catholic Encyclopedia Second Edition (15 vol. set). Waterville, ME: Gale Group, 2002.

Bob O'Gorman and Mary Faulkner, *The Complete Idiot's Guide to Understanding Catholicism*. 2nd ed. New York: Alpha Books, 2003.

Rev. John Trigilio Jr. and Rev. Kenneth Brighenti, *Understanding Catholicism*. Hoboken, NJ: Wiley Publishing, Inc., 2003.

History of the Catholic Church

Judith A. Bauer, ed., *The Essential Mary Handbook: A Summary of Beliefs, Practices, and Prayers*. Liguori, MO: Liguori Publications, 1999.

Tessa Bielecki, *Teresa of Avila: Mystical Writings*. New York: Crossroad/Herder & Herder, 1994.

Leonard Boff, *Ecclesiogenesis: The Base Communities Reinvent the Church*. Maryknoll, NY: Orbis Books, 1986.

Joan D. Chittister, *The Rule of Benedict: Insights for the Ages*. New York: Crossroad/Herder & Herder, 1992.

Kathy Coffey, *Hidden Women of the Gospels*. Maryknoll, NY: Orbis Books, 2003.

Oliver Davies and Fiona Bowie, *Celtic Christian Spirituality: An Anthology of Medieval and Modern Sources*. New York: Continuum, 1999.

Cyprian Davies, *The History of Black Catholics in the United States*. New York: Crossroad/Herder & Herder, 1995.

Jay P. Dolan, *In Search of an American Catholicism*. New York: Oxford University Press, 2002.

Avery Dulles, *Models of the Church*. New York: Image Books, 1991.

Virgilio P. Elizondo, *Guadalupe: Mother of the New Creation*. Maryknoll, NY: Orbis Books, 1997.

Mary Faulkner, *Supreme Authority: Understanding Power in the Catholic Church*. Indianapolis: Alpha Books, 2002.

Paul Giles, *American Catholic Arts and Fictions: Culture, Ideology, Aesthetics*. New York: Cambridge University Press, 1992.

Andrew Greeley, *The Catholic Imagination*. Berkeley: University of California Press, 2001.

Andrew Greeley, *The Catholic Myth: The Behavior and Beliefs of American Catholics*. New York: Collier Books, 1997.

Thomas Groome, *What Makes Us Catholic: Eight Gifts for Life*. San Francisco: Harper San Francisco, 2003.

Monika K. Hellwig, *Understanding Catholicism*. Mahwah, NJ: Paulist Press, 2002.

W. Heywood, ed., *The Little Flowers of St. Francis of Assisi*. New York: Vintage Books, 1998.

Hugo Hoever, *Lives of the Saints for Every Day of the Year*. New York: Catholic Book Pub. Co., 1999.

Francois Icher, *Building the Great Cathedrals*. New York: Abradale Press, 2001.

Hans Kung, *The Catholic Church: A Short History*. New York: Modern Library, 2003.

Mark Stephen Massa, *Catholics and American Culture: Fulton Sheen, Dorothy Day, and the Notre Dame Football Team*. New York: Crossroad/Herder & Herder, 1999.

Mary J. F. C. Meara, Jeffrey Λ. J. Stone, Maureen A. T. Kelly, and Richard G. M. Davis, *Growing Up Catholic: An Infinitely Funny Guide for the Faithful, the Fallen and Everyone In-Between*. New York: Broadway Books, 2000.

Charles Morris, *American Catholic: The Saints and Sinners Who Built America's Most Powerful Church*. New York: Vintage Books, 1998.

Robert T. O'Gorman, *The Church That Was a School: Catholic Identity and Catholic Education in the United States Since 1790*. Washington, DC: The Catholic Education Futures Project, 1987.

Annette Sandoval, *The Directory of Saints: A Concise Guide to Patron Saints*. New York: Penguin Books, 1997.

Joseph A. Tetlow, *Ignatius Loyola: Spiritual Exercises*. New York: Crossroad/Herder & Herder, 1992.

Mary R. Thompson, *Mary of Magdala: Apostle and Leader*. Mahwah, NJ: Paulist Press, 1995.

Greg Tobin, *Saints and Sinners: The American Catholic Experience Through Stories, Memoirs, Essays and Commentary*. New York: Doubleday, 1999.

Cletus Wessels, *The Holy Web: Church and the New Universe Story*. Maryknoll, NY: Orbis Books, 2000.

Gerry Wills, *Why I Am a Catholic*. Boston: Houghton Mifflin Co., 2002.

Index